2016
THE BEST
WOMEN'S STAGE MONOLOGUES

2016
THE BEST
WOMEN'S STAGE MONOLOGUES

Edited by
Lawrence Harbison

SMITH AND KRAUS PUBLISHERS   2016

ISBN: 1-57525-906-0
ISBN: 978-1-57525-906-2
ISSN: 2329-2709

Typesetting and layout by Elizabeth Monteleone
Cover Design: Olivia Monteleone

A Smith and Kraus book
177 Lyme Road, Hanover, NH 03755
Editorial 603.643.6431 To Order 1.877.668.8680
www.smithandkraus.com

Printed in the United States of America

TABLE OF CONTENTS

Lawrence Harbison

FOREWORD

Here you will find a rich and varied selection of monologues for women from plays which were produced and/or published in the 2015-2016 theatrical season. Many are for younger performers (teens through 30s) but there are also some excellent pieces for older women as well. Some are comic (laughs), some are dramatic (generally, no laughs). Some are rather short, some are rather long. All represent the best in contemporary playwriting.

Several of the monologues are by playwrights whose work may be familiar to you, such as Don Nigro, Lisa D'Amour, Dominique Morisseau, John Pollono, Saviana Stanescu and Deborah Zoe Laufer; others are by exciting up-and-comers such as Nicole Pandolfo, Emily Schwend, Fengar Gael, Abby Rosebrock, Max Baker, Maura Campbell and Jacqueline Goldfinger.

Many of the plays from which these monologues have been culled have been published and, hence, are readily available either from the publisher/licensor or from a theatrical book store such as the Drama Book Shop in New York. A few plays may not be published for a while, in which case contact the author or his agent to request a copy of the entire text of the play which contains the monologue which suits your fancy. Information on publishers/rights holders may be found in the Rights & Permissions section in the back of this anthology.

Break a leg in that audition! Knock 'em dead in class!

Lawrence Harbison

Dramatic
Reader, an African American woman past middle age.

Here, she describes to the viewer the limits to the possible characters she can play, and how she transitions from one to the other.

READER: Identity. I put on my hat, I become Miz Bee, the widowed schoolteacher, accentuating my final "g's" so as never to be confused with the riff-raff on the corner. "*Everythin'. Nothin'.*" With my nice leather bag from Bloomingdales, to remind there are rewards, my every five years weeklong excursion to Paris, France, where I can say "Toor Eefel" with the best of them. I put on this wig, I become Naomi Johnson, social worker. And this (*pointing to a gray veil like an a beekeeper's*) well, maybe that'll be later. But when it comes to shape-shifting, it seems I don't have much range. I wind up playing the gatekeeper—adoption bureau, civil servant. The year is 1968, and you can only be what you have seen, even if only in the mind's eye. But when I go to Leroy's and take my rum 'n coke, I don't see myself in those horns. Except in some woozy reflection laughing at me, at the very idea of me. The horns, that's what calls to me, though in my father's house, we played only Chopin. The alphabet? That's a natural role, I suppose. I've been teaching it so long. A slave could get killed for learning it, and a free man could get killed for teaching it. So that's the little piece of the load I carry, lifting it up. You'd think that from the alphabet, it'd be easy, just a hop, skip and and a jump to combining letters, an infinite array of possibilities. But we can only be what we have seen. It's 1968. A couple of years ago, Mr. Watson and Mr. Crick won the Nobel prize for configuring DNA as a spiral. Soon we will recombine and recompose, faces with a hundred fingers, a woman in the shape of a dragon. Soon we can be anything. But not yet.

Dramatic

Miz Bee, elderly African American

Miz Bee: Of course, here I am testifying to you, but am I following my own advice? No, I'm drinking. In fact, I think I'll have another one of those rum 'n cokes. Thinking about Jerome. Seems like liquor takes the edge off till Jesus can come round 'n take the pain. I don't believe in those pills they give you for your feelings. A prescription on white paper for white pills from a nurse in a white uniform. This here's brown. It's my home medicine.

Barack, now—that's like a miracle. I never thought to see this day. When we used to go down in the summer to see my mother's people in Carolina—the things I seen—And they don't tell you none of that in *Eyes on the Prize*! They say there was separate water fountains and bathrooms, but they don't tell you a lot of the stops there were no colored restrooms. And my big brother would say "Don't drink, don't drink," but I couldn't help it, I got so thirsty! And we'd be doing the bee dance, hopping from foot to foot. And at each station "is there a colored restroom?" and "No—dang it!" and the train'd just go on and on. We had to go so bad! One time I wet myself, and I just sitting there on that hard train seat all stinky, and my mother said "Aren't you ashamed of yourself?" But I couldn't help it. Must've been five, six hundred miles without a rest stop. Or felt like it, anyway. And now this! Barack. That is God's grace that I would live to see the day. Everybody so happy. And I'm the bad fairy at the picnic. On account of Jerome. Shot in the back. Just playing in the street. Five years old. My godson. Cutest thing. Just out playing, never did harm to nobody. Just caught in the crossfire. I been thinking about your brother even before

I run into you, Zafiya. Tyrone. Jerome. Even the names sound the same. They say he's gonna be all right. Well, not all right, he's shot in the spine. Maybe he'll walk. Maybe he'll be some kind of plegic—paraplegic, quad-riplegic. But they got metal now, they've got medical wonders—I've been reading. They implant a circuit and you spark yourself into life just by flicking your tongue. He's gonna live by God's grace, and it's God's grace you and I met here tonight, Zafiya…

(She breaks down.)

A black man in the White House! Black slaves *built* that house. Five hundred miles and never a place to stop and rest. God's grace. And Jerome … I need another drink.

Seriocomic
Tanya, sixty-two

> *Tanya is a hooker, working out of the Humming Bird,*
> *a fleabag motel in New Orleans. She's had a life of*
> *hard knocks but she still looks pretty good for her age.*
> *Zoe, a teenager there for a visit with her mother's boy*
> *toy Bait Boy, who used to live there, is writing a paper*
> *for school, some sort of anthropological study, and is*
> *interviewing the residents of the motel. Tanya tells her*
> *about the motel and its denizens.*

TANYA: That's right baby you are at the HUMMING BIRD
and we may be a little rough around the edges but if
there is one thing we know how to do, it is throw down
a party. That's right it's Jazz Fest and our dear friend is
sunsetting and needs to be celebrated. Because people
don't celebrate enough in this life – they let things roll
by unnoticed, which is why it's good you are doing your
little paper sweetie – Don't let Sissy Na Na scare you,
you are a good little student we're glad you decided to
come out here and notice us. I mean how would this city
SURVIVE without us? Who's gonna serve those belliger-
ent frat boys drinks? Who's gonna make sure the whole
slutty bachelorette party gets up on stage for the booty
dance? Who's gonna serve the half-drunk housewife from
Charlotte "Sex on the Beach" out of a test tube you are
holding in your cleavage? Celebrate, you hear me? Cause
we had to go down a long strange road to be who we are
– a road filled with construction and roadkill and booby
traps and scam artists and bad decisions masquerading
as good decisions and bad luck masquerading as good
luck and bad friends masquerading as good friends and
treachery lurking around every corner, and you just stay

on the road – Looking for an exit, and when you realize there is no exit you get out and start walking – You start walking and you keep walking, along the edge of the highway, with no idea of where you're going or where you belong, Until one morning the sun rises and you find yourself here. And there is no one else like us in the whole world.

For information on this author, click on the WRITERS tab at www.smithandkraus.com.

Comic
Marie, twenties to forties, African American

> *Marie and her siblings are in a park, awaiting the
> arrival of their sister, upon whom they plan to do an
> intervention. While waiting, she reminisces about a
> gruesome murder which took place in their neighbor-
> hood.*

MARIE: We was all at the house on Baltimore. And Mama
had just started batterin' some chicken and Big Bob
came runnin in shoutin'- "HE KILLED MAMA HE
KILLED MAMA!" And I was like "WHO KILLED
WHO??!!" And Big Bob was like "WHOOKIE
JUST KILLED MAMA!!" Then all of a sudden the rest
of Big Bob's brothers and sisters come running into the
damn house with blood all over their arms and stuff
and I'm like "WAIT A GATDAMN MINUTE WHATS
GOIN' ONS???" *(laughing)* And they all started talkin
real fast real quick and we all ran out to the porch and
they pointed across the street at their house. It was
funny. *(beat)* So of course me, Tina, Tyrone, Melvin,
Terry and Alphonso, we take our curious asses on over
there to see what was what and when we get there we
walk into the kitchen and see Whookie standing there
smoking a cigarette with his mama's head *sitting* on the
counter next to him... Her *body* on the floor and her *head*
on the counter. Blood everywhere... and Whookie was
real cool just talking to her like ain't nothing was nothing. "I told you to give me a gatdamn cigarette. I ain't
gat time for no damn games mama. Now you see. *Now*
you see. All you have to do is give me a gatdamn cigarette and we be cool." This crazy fool chopped his

---

own mama's head off cuz she refused to give him her last damn cigarette. Ya'll remember.

For information on this author, click on the WRITERS tab at www.smithandkraus.com.

Dramatic
Adlean, thirties to forties, African American

> *Adlean and her siblings have come together in a park
> to do an intervention on their sister, Barbara. They
> have tied her to a tree and put tape opver her mother
> so she will have to listen to them. Here, Adlean pleads
> with Barbara to go into rehab.*

ADLEAN: Barbara... I remember how you use to come in
and... tickle my feet in the morning. You knew I never
liked getting up for school so you said you'd wake me up
with a laugh. And I know sometimes I'd bust you in the
jaw with a shoe... but the ticklin' grew on me and I started
to expect it... Well Barbara... I need my little tickle alarm
clock back in my life. I would like to leave this earth
knowing that you had gotten your life back together...
put your self together in a whole different way without
all those drugs and drink. It makes me very sad to have to
be riding through downtown with my grandkids and see
you standing on the street corner after having shitted on
yourself. That one time I stopped... it broke my heart to
see you. But you should know I have not stopped many
many many times Barbara. The time you were riding
on the front of that old man's Hoveround wheelchair. In
the middle of the street. The time you were chasing
down some wimmen with a hot glue gun and no draws on
your ass. Ass just in the air. In the middle of the street. I
said to myself. "Is that my sister Barbara? In the middle
of the gatdamn street?" ...I don't stop anymore. For the
sake of my grandkids I don't stop. But Zippity Boom
you have to stop. *You* need help, Barbara. We've found
a place that can help you. We will be here to support you
when you return. Barbara, will you please take this gift

we are giving you. We love you. Will you please go to rehab, Barbara? Will you please take this help from those nice people up there in Alaska?

For information on this author, click on the WRITERS tab at www.smithandkraus.com.

Dramatic
Marie, twenties to forties, African American

> *Marie and her siblings are in a park doing an intervention on their sister, Barbara, Whom they call "Zippity Boom" and who they have tied to a tree and put tape over her mouth so she will have to listen to them.*

MARIE: Barbara... Zippity Boom... *(sings)* "Sistah you been on my mind"... *(beat)* You remember when you and me and Lillie Anne and Adlean and Tina we all went out and had us a girls night out? We went to that little club downtown on the corner of Grafton. What was it called? I think it was Kellers. Remember. We had to sneak Tina in cuz she had just turned 16 or something. We all sat up in there like we was grown and dared anybody to tell us any different... You had your first pina colada. And we could tell you liked it. Cuz that was the day we met Zippity Boom. Zippity Boom Boom. She came OUT that night for the first time and we was all laughing. We use to *laugh*, Barbara. Remember. Just all night. Remember when we gat back from Kellers that night... we snuck in through the side window and we had to almost smother you to keep you from laughing too loud and waking up mama and daddy... and we all just decided to sleep in the same bed... *sistahs... togetha...* we woke up just like that in the morning... *togetha... woke up...* from a bucket of ice cold water being thrown on us... looked down and saw that we were all tied to one another remember? Mama standing there ... empty bucket in one hand and in the other hand she had that green water hose she had cut in half... remember that... that green snake whip... she proceeded to beat the hell out of all of us... and you...

Zippity Boom... you just kept right on laughing... I want my sister back...

For information on this author, click on the WRITERS tab at www.smithandkraus.com.

Dramatic
Janice, forty

> *Janice is a seasoned police detective pursuing a serial*
> *killer who strangled eight women and buried their*
> *bodies on a remote beach. She is an alcoholic. In this*
> *scene, she is speaking to Cass, an ex-con, and a suspect*
> *in the investigation. The two are smoking cigarettes*
> *outside a bar, and Janice has been provoking Cass,*
> *hoping for a reaction. She has had a lot to drink, but*
> *holds her liquor well.*

JANICE: When a person is strangled, the hyoid is broken. It's the telltale sign. And the bodies we found out there – every one of them. Broken hyoid. Seven young women. All with a crushed hyoid. Except one. The eighth body. The anomaly. She was found a little ways away from the others. She was the most recently buried. And she didn't have a crushed hyoid. She had injuries to her neck, she'd been strangled. But that's not what killed her. It was the three gunshot wounds to her chest that did that. We found her in the scrub grass near the road. She was closer to the highway than the others. All of the bodies were buried near the shore, and the oldest ones were closest to the water. In a line, more or less. Which makes me think. Every big storm, a little more of the island washes away. Water level gets higher. What else has been washed away? More bodies? Out in the ocean now, disintegrated? We found eight. How many more are out there? How many will this storm wash away tonight? Fifty years, a hundred years, a hundred fifty….eventually the whole island's gonna be under water. Then who will care? Who killed who. Why. Where's the body at.

Was there justice. We're Atlantis. A city underwater that maybe never existed at all.

For information on this author, click on the WRITERS tab at www.smithandkraus.com.

Dramatic
Janice, forty

> *Janice is a seasoned detective speaking to her younger,*
> *less experienced partner Ted. The two are involved in*
> *a serial murder investigation. Janice is an alcoholic*
> *and is struggling to keep functioning. Earlier this year*
> *she had three toes amputated, and has never given a*
> *straight answer as to why. In this scene, Ted comes*
> *to Janice's apartment at 5 pm, to find her asleep and*
> *hung-over. He confronts her about how she lost her toes.*

JANICE: Ted, you've got this romanticized notion of confession. Very Catholic. That unburdening yourself offers some sort of release. Absolution. That it'll make everything better. This notion that if you open the floodgates, then the pressure is eased, there's some kind of purification. That's not how it works. If I share my shit with you, it just means there's shit on both of us. It's why I can't stand AA. Non-stop shit-smearing. I don't like sharing. And I don't like others sharing with me. Last February. Bartender took my car keys, so I had to walk home. It was cold, but I barely felt it. I got home, realized my house keys are on the same keychain as my car keys. I don't keep a key hidden outside. I should have broken a window, called you, done anything to get inside, but I wasn't thinking clearly. I'm standing there by my door, wondering what I should do, and I really need to pee. And then I wet my pants. So I thought, "Well, fuck, this sucks, I'm exhausted. I'm going to sleep." So I passed out on my front porch. When I woke up in the morning, it really was freezing, and I knew my foot was fucked. Turns out all the pee had gone down one leg and collected in my shoe. The pee froze overnight. By morning the toes were frozen stiff. I could barely get the shoe off. The ER doctor said he had to amputate three of them. And here I am. I feel better. Now, not only do I have to live with that, but I also have the comforting knowledge that you know. That I crippled myself in the stupidest, most degrading way possible. I feel much better.

For information on this author, click on the WRITERS tab at www.smithandkraus.com.

Dramatic
Caithleen, twenty

> *Caithleen is a tour guide in Dublin, specializing in James Joyce's Dublin. She is talking to Robert, a 55 year-old American, whom she has never met – or has she? Is he, in fact, her boyfriend Robbie, 35 years later?*

CAITHLEEN: Okay - you tell me. Right now. You tell me to my face: how do you know these things about me? I bet my Da put you up to this! He as much as admitted to it - the other night - my Dad - rolled home from the pub stinkin' of smoke and the perfume of some Hatch Street whore. Said *"Don't tempt me, Caithleen – 'cause I'll do it! I'll drum up a way to scare you straight - so you won't end up like your lunatic mother."* He had her committed, you know. They hauled her away to St. Brendan's. My Da - my Dad did that to her! - but I bet you know that - I bet he told you things about me - things to make me scared - make me feel like I'm going mad like my Ma did .That's how it started with her, you know: Time stopped behavin' like it should. Things in the past or future refused to stay where they belonged. People started showin' up in her days and they'd be the *wrong age.* An' no matter how much I told her "it's a dream Mama, it's an odd stray thought of a thing" - no, she wouldn't be put off the idea - not at all - till she was so scared - scared of people showing up *with no regard to the time it was in their lives.* An' she kept seein' *a boy with wild black hair* - an' she kept sayin' *"I know what that boy's gonna do one day!"* - oh, she'd pray an' she'd moan an' that's when my Da would come in an' put an end to things with a hard open hand. *Pause.* I don't want to be her. End up like her. Do I?

For information on this author, click on the WRITERS tab at www.smithandkraus.com.

Dramatic
Bonnie, twenty-seven

> *Bonnie Hill is thrilled to have corralled her sister,*
> *Corey and future sister in laws, Kayleigh and Larissa*
> *into celebrating her engagement with a hotel getaway*
> *weekend. She is genuinely in awe of her fiancé and*
> *explains to the other women how he proposed.*

BONNIE: It was so simple and romantic. We drove up to
Asheville actually up to one of those lookouts. It was
super sweet because you know how normally I don't
love nature? So, well we didn't have to walk that far
and the view was just … unrelenting. I can't even. It
literally took my breath away. Which may have been
the altitude. But. He got down on one knee with all
these blossoms and flowers and the sun low in the
sky behind him. All I could think about was, remember that bumper sticker daddy had that said "Spring
Has Sprung?" and it had that enormous flower jumping
on a trampoline, like catapulting into the sky? Well
that's how Austin looked, just this burst of color, like
exploding behind him, just like my heart was exploding into my throat and like, his words were so calm
and quiet, "will, you, marry, me" but the colors behind him were just...so loud and so certain. Just like
I felt. And I said, equally quietly, as certain as the sun
was bright, es. Of course" I mean, I almost just blurted
"Duh, Austin, DUH!" But like, obviously not. Just the
quietest "Yes." And that was it. It was done. I feel like
one of those results of an anthropological study where
it's like I went out into the wilderness and I found the
most capable man and I just... owned him. You know?

So anyway. That's how it happened.

For information on this author, click on the
WRITERS tab at www.smithandkraus.com.

Dramatic
Beth, late forties

> *Beth is confronting her husband Tommy's friend
> Fletcher Driscoll. Tommy is a charming control
> freak and bully who emotionally and sexually abused
> Fletcher thirty years ago and who currently emotionally
> manipulates and dominates his wife. Tommy has told
> her that Fletcher is still in love with him (a lie, but she
> doesn't know that) and she's bothered enough by it to
> seek Fletcher out, even though Tommy expressly asked
> her not to. They play she refers to is a production of
> Romeo & Juliet Fletcher has returned to town to direct.*

BETH: Tommy told me what happened. He didn't want to
but... He felt I should know how you... How you con-
fessed to him when you saw him a few weeks ago...
that you were in love with him when you were in high
school... And that you still are. It's all right. I don't blame
you. If anyone knows what it's like to be in love with
Tommy, it's me. He's such a strong person. So smart
and accomplished. And so handsome. And I know I'm
not... I'm not special. I know how lucky I am to have
him. But you have to accept that you can't. *(Pause)* I'm
not angry. If anything, I'm concerned. Deeply. Thirty
years a long time to cling to someone you can never
have. I don't mean to sound like I'm staking any sort of
claim. I know I don't have to do that. My husband loves
me. And even if he didn't... He could never do anything
with another man. So these feelings you have for him...
You need to let go of them. They're not doing you any
good and... Anyway, I think it's only appropriate that I
decline your very generous offer to see the play on opening night. Tommy isn't really that interested, but I have
to see it for my poetry class, so I think it would be best

if I attended after you were no longer here. And if you would please not contact my husband again... that would also be for the best.

For information on this author, click on the WRITERS tab at www.smithandkraus.com.

Dramatic
Amanda Clifford, late 40s

> *Amanda is confronting her ex-husband Jeff, 52. They
> split because after fourteen years of marriage, Jeff
> finally accepted that he was gay and wanted to live hon-
> estly. Amanda recently realized that Jeff was probably
> in love with her brother Ellis, who introduced them.
> Ellis passed away two years ago today and they are
> at his gravesite. When Ellis was sick, Jeff stood by her
> and has been nothing but supportive throughout their
> ordeals, which has made it difficult for her to be angry
> with him. She's finally letting it all out.*

AMANDA: Fuck you. *(pause)* Fuck. You. Your life wasn't the
only one you wasted because you didn't know who the
hell you were! And in the meantime, I'm supposed to be
happy for you? To support this "voyage of discovery"? I
know we haven't been around each other much over the
past year. But every time we have, I see it. You're losing weight and working out and... whatever! And I feel
stupid that it makes me angry because... I never wanted
you to "improve yourself." I loved you as you were. So,
you know what I've been thinking about since we had our
little discussion? How Ellis described you to me when
he was trying to set us up. I'll never forget it. "Cute in a
middle-aged professor sort of way, has a face that'll look
really handsome if he loses some weight." How was I to
know that when you actually hit middle age, you'd stop
looking like a middle-aged professor in order to make
yourself attractive to other men, especially another man
who looks so much like (Ellis)?

Part of me wishes you had just been a bastard, or run off
and left me hanging, or had done something unforgive-
able. Even now... now that you've done something that

I should not be able to forgive... I still can't hate you! Because when I do the math, I realize that while I was in a dead-end relationship with you, you were in a dead-end relationship with him.

(Points to the grave.)

None of us got what we wanted. So I can be angry now. And I can hate you now. But sooner rather than later, that anger and hatred are going to go away. And I am going to miss it.

For information on this author, click on the WRITERS tab at www.smithandkraus.com.

Dramatic
Siomara, thirties

> *Siomara is speaking to herself in this monologue as she opens the box that has lived – forever locked – on her family's mantle. She doesn't quite understand it, but she is being driven to unlock her family's secrets before she can face the baby she is newly pregnant with. In this scene, she has just stolen and smashed the box on her parent's mantle. As she takes out and looks at its contents, she realizes she has to go break Cuba open as well, go back to Cuba, in order to truly understand that long, slippery trail her parent's migration from the island left in its wake. This is also a scene in which Siomara discovers her grandfather is black. This is significant to her, among other reasons, because her husband is African American.*

SIOMARA: *(holding a picture up)* My mother. My mother with an enormous gun. A soldier? A warrior? Harsh. Battle written all over her face. Her knee up on a rock and her hair cropped short. The Marquesa ... with a gun like a fucking penis jutting from her pelvis. I don't know my mother. I have no idea who my mother is.

(Takes another picture.)

My father, barechested, catching fish.

(Picking up other pictures)

Him and tio Dio as children by the sea.

(Arm extended towards another picture, picks it up.)

A man behind them in one of the pictures. The way his arm is wrapped around them. So tender. Is that my grandfather? Could that be...?

(She stares at this one for a while.)

He's dark; black as night. But not the urban night, darker, like night in the country—his eyes like two bold stars, one for each of his sons. And then a picture of the same man I think is my grandfather, on stilts. Dressed to the hilt in some fabulous costume, towering over the crowds that watch him. He›s bending over and giving my father a flower; my father standing there looking at this man like this man is God. Dad, barefoot and with a smile that looks like it›s going to tear through his face and mark the world with the purest kind of joy, that joy that's made of love.

(a shift, dropping all the pictures from her hands)

Swim there...Swim to Cuba—it's all that goes through my head, and I think: the only thing left to do is jump. Jump in the water and swim backwards. The goal is singular, and like I'm an animal: do what your father can't; what he's too much of a coward to do; follow the brightest light, the stars in your dead grandfather's eyes. Swim back, all the way back to Cuba. Figure it all out. Find your father's Bonsai. Trim it. See where you come from. The soil that took the seeds that made your family, that made you ... And then the water becomes too much. She starts to drown me. Harsh. I can't catch my breath. The water. Is. Sharp as a shark. Biting.

For information on this author, click on the WRITERS tab at www.smithandkraus.com.

Dramatic
Tabby, thirties

> *Tabby has risen to the top of her deceased father's company. She tells Graham, her main rival and nemesis, that she is sacking him.*

TABBY: Hi Graham. Welcome to my shiny new office. What do you think? You've been a loyal servant of this company for so many years, you must have seen a few changes. I bet, for example, that you never expected to see me here. In this office. In this Very. Nice. Chair. No. In fact I think you've had *your* beady eye on this office for some time. But there we are. That's the way the cookie arse-fucks you. Right? Please. Have a seat. I'm joking. Stand the fuck up. God. Now. Graham. Before we go any further allow me to make one thing clear I appreciate the way you looked out for me after Daddy died. Taught me the tricks of the trade as it were. You really took me under your wing. Well. Your desk. You did me quite a few favours. You taught me everything I needed to know: do this, do that, suck this, touch that. Yes I think I can still taste your 'favours'. But look at me now. And look at you. OK enough of that Graham, we can do this the hard way. Or we can do this the abject Excruciating Horrifying way. Oh come on you must have seen this coming. You must appreciate your position here has now become untenable. Don't Oh don't cry Graham for God's sake. I'm fucking you this time. Take it like a man.

Dramatic
Eve, mid-teens

> *Eve lives in squalor in Tabby's house. We think Tabby is*
> *her sister; later, we find out that Tabby is actually her*
> *mother. Eve is a very disturbed girl who thinks she's a*
> *vampire. Here, while waiting for Tabby to come home,*
> *she talks to the audience.*

EVE: Sometimes I see footprints. Little bare feet. One left
one right. Shining. Like snail trails. They walk across the
floor up the wall and across the ceiling and down the wall
and then. Out. Under the door. And then I realise they are
my footprints. And I follow them. Out of the safe place.
Out through the castle. Past the walls. Out of Loughton.
Into Albion. Into the Wild Places. I can walk for miles.
Into the mists and the marshes where the giants' daughters
walk. The short cracked shouts of unseen hook-beaked
birds. Where the plants and earth shiver with business.
Of millions of things living their short amazing lives The
sunshine feels like warm water on my skin. I tread on
soft green meadows. Clutch wet earth with my toes. Ride
with the wild white horses and scatter the birds before
me. Watch them warble and rise shrieking. I stick to the
path through the trees. Though the wolf tempts me. His
thick hair bristles and hot damp breaths. Claws scrape
on my skin. Under my clothes. He touches my bad bits
and we howl. I pick the larkspur and forget-me—not;
the monkshood and snow-on-the-mountain. And I put
them in my hair. I could walk the world. South to scale
Mount Olympus or north to the frozen mouth of Gin-
nungagap. East to the Great Wall or West to Ground Zero
and the Gap in the Sky. Or I could just wander. Through
the tree lands. Tabby and me. Where the people aren't

afraid and no one wants to kill me. And everyone who passes by I just smile. And they smile back. And I can ask them questions and touch Them. And then they. . . they touch me too.

Dramatic
Devon, eighteen

> *Devon Tramore, a woman jockey, lies on a hospital bed,*
> *recovering from a fall that resulted in broken bones and*
> *a severe concussion. The race in which she fell might*
> *have been sabotaged, so the Louisiana Racing Com-*
> *mission Inspector, a middle-aged woman, is questioning*
> *her regarding the social dynamics of the jockey room.*

DEVON: What do you think it's like in the jockey's room? Me and ten jocks with valets and agents and the press coming and going, all of them guys and all of them thinking they're god's gift. When I started here two years ago, I was sixteen and had a crush on half the jocks riding, so if you're asking did I flirt, then yeah, at first I smiled and whistled when they walked around naked, but I didn't screw around, and it's not that I never wanted to. 'Course the ones I liked blew me off, and the rest were total creeps. Seriously, some of those guys are like a wolf pack and I'm the chicken, and there's nothing girls can do but wait till they die off and hope the next batch come out better. You wouldn't believe the stunts they pulled to get rid of me: spreading rumors that I'm a nympho who gets mounts by jerking off trainers, or putting catfish in my locker and spying on me in the shower, but mostly they just acted like I wasn't even there. Look, bottom line: I fell off Senor Pepe and nearly croaked, but his damn hospital with all their drugs and high tech shit can't do fuck all, so I'm healing myself. Sure, at first I hated Ellis and the whole fuckin' world 'cause I thought I was through, but now I know I'll be riding long after that lowlife's retired, and just you wait: I'm going to be the first woman to win a grade one stakes in Louisiana, and I'll keep breaking records — so if you're a gambler, don't forget me 'cause I've got a future: I'm going to get well and win so many races, they'll have to build a new wing on the house to hold all my trophies! Someday soon, all the best trainers will be begging me to ride their horses at every track in the country. I'll need my own private jet, 'cause I'll be flying to fan clubs in all fifty states full of girls even younger than me and smaller too — 'cause even though size is everything in this macho man's world, it's our turn to rule and be cool! There's no stopping us now, and you'll see: there'll be so many wonder women jockeys and trainers, we're going to shake up the sport of kings till they call it the sport of *(whinnying)* queeeeee hee hee heeeens!!

For information on this author, click on the WRITERS tab at www.smithandkraus.com.

Seriocomic
Marya, late twenties

> *The great Russian novelist Dostoyevsky, serving out
> the last four years of his sentence for treason in the
> military in Siberia, has fallen desperately in love with
> a beautiful but troubled married woman, Marya, whose
> drunken and sometimes brutal husband has made her
> life hell, dragged her to this remote location in the
> middle of nowhere, then lost his job and is now drink-
> ing himself to death. She knows that Dostoyevsky is in
> love with her, but hesitates to get involved with him,
> both because she knows her husband might kill him,
> and because Dostoyevsky is a very strange and rather
> alarming person himself. Marya is intelligent, nervous,
> perceptive, has trouble concentrating, is very funny, is
> aware of her beauty and her power over men, is not
> cruel but is very honest, and isn't sure what she wants.
> In short, she is exactly the sort of person to drive the
> earnest and self-sabotaging Dostoyevsky absolutely
> berserk with unhappiness. She can see this but can't
> seem to help it.*

MARYA: My crime was marrying a drunkard who dragged
me to Siberia so he could be a customs official. He
thought it would be a smart career move to take a dull job
that pays next to nothing on the backside of the universe,
then quit and take up drinking full time. Now he spends
all night drinking and all day looking for a job where
they'll pay him to drink. He's a drunken imbecile. I can't
remember why I married him. I must have been having a
psychotic episode. I married below my station, and now
I can't get off the train. My father believed his daughters
should be well educated, so we spent a lot of time reading

Kant and playing the piano, which is as much use to me here as a piano would be to a goat. Although I suppose a goat could eat a piano if he was hungry enough. My next musical composition: "Goat Eating A Grand Piano." It comes after "Grand Piano Falling Out Of Third Story Window" and before "Grand Piano Eating A Goat." I'm so desperately bored I have no idea what I'm saying. But you're unhappy, too. Unhappy people are drawn to each other like magnets. You'd better stay away from me, or you'll fall in love with me, and since you can't have me, you'll want to kill yourself, but instead you'll write a novel. Out here, everything is so ugly and stupid, and the women are so ugly and stupid, that the men, who are also ugly and stupid, all decide they're in love with me. It's a curse...Men are good at making promises. It's nothing personal I have against you. It's just that I'm incapable of love. Not of passion. I'm capable of passion. Even lust. But not love. And only for the wrong person. I've been damaged by life. So have you, of course. Life is an ongoing series of disasters culminating in a catastrophe which is usually an anti-climax. So be in love with me if you must. But please do me the courtesy of not hanging yourself.

Dramatic
Shelly, forty-five, African American

> *Shelly tells Jackie, an old friend from the neighborhood,*
> *that her mother. Dotty, has incipient dementia and it's*
> *getting to be too much for her to handle.*

SHELLY: It's dementia.   She was diagnosed, what, about a
year ago? But she's been hiding this from us for a while.
I just thought she was just getting forgetful, you know.
But then, one day, I got a call at my office that she got
pulled over for driving, like, 95 miles an hour on Kelly
Drive around all those curves and bends. When the cop
asked why she was driving so fast, she said that "the
wind felt good on her"— The cop asked where she was
going and...and...she didn't know. She had no idea where
she was going. They found my number as one of the last
numbers dialed in her phone and called me. I came and
picked her up from the police station down on Girard
Avenue. Now you know, I don't go down on Girard
Avenue. It was such a scene as I am trying to verify that
she is my mother and then she freaked out and cussed
EVERYBODY out and they had the paramedics take her
to the hospital and deal with all THAT and then they
kept her for a few days and did all of these tests and then
the questions about her health and sanity and well, they
told me that it was dementia. And it has just been getting worse every day. I just can't let her be in this house
alone. I am afraid of what she will get into or forget to
do. For the past few weeks, I've had to take her with
me to work. On Friday, she drove me so crazy trying to
organize my files at my office. Said she was trying to
help. I come in from a staff meeting and she is pointing
to a crazy looking file, telling me to take a hard look at

it. Looks like she made this file with newspaper articles and a whole lot of random chaos. CHAOS! I'm telling you, one minute she is so lucid, remembering names of mayors of 1953 and the next she doesn't remember what she asked one minute ago. On Halloween I think she told me that she planned on killing herself. Well not in those words. She said, "I don't ever want to be a burden to anyone. I will go when I am in control of it! I won't linger and be a burden." The way her mind works, she probably forgot she said that. But you can't be too sure. So I'm watching.

Comic
Averie, thirty-five, African American

> *Averie has appeared on a couple of reality TV shows.*
> *She's busted, though, and is living in her sister Shelly's*
> *basement. Shelly has asked her and their brother Don-*
> *nie to come over to talk about what to do about their*
> *mother's incipient dementia; but Averie is more inter-*
> *ested in telling everyone about a new show she's up for.*

AVERIE: Y'all can talk about chitlins all you want but you
know you love 'em. Yes, they may stink up the house
for a good 48 hours but they are a delicacy. That is all
the slaves could eat. Everything that the slave masters
didn't want and threw away and our people had to make
something out of it to survive. Fatback, snouts, ears,
neck bones, feet, and intestines, given to the slaves. You
gotta take lemons and make some shit out of it. And if you
don't ... well ... I don't know what to tell you. My new
agent called me today and said that I am up for Celebrity
Mud Fight. I know what y'all are going to say, but let
me tell you, it's a good opportunity. To make some real
money!!! CELEBRITY MUD FIGHT! Every week we
would mud fight to stay in the house. And no, there is
no prize money but it is a chance that would lead to
financial opportunities. No need for the side-eye Shelly.
Ask Donnie! He knows about a brand. He writes those
plays about race and sexuality and he is always talking
about it when he does his interviews. His brand. Wearing
those glasses and speaking so intelligently! It's branding.
And I am about to get mine on! I have taken the scraps up
off the floor and made lemonade out of it. Chitlins. Clean
'em, boil the hell out of 'em with a little baking soda and
salt. Season 'em up and what? Delicious! Lynnie Poo

down the street, even goes so far as to throw them in the washing machine for the final rinse. Now that's crazy! She also makes bath soap out of pot liquor from collard greens but that's another story! We gonna have some pork chitlins, not Chitterlings, for Christmas, because momma said she missed her mamma's chiltin's and that's what she's gonna get. And no, they didn't come from no Whole Foods, Donnie, and they are not organic, Adam. We are having regular ole chitlins for mom and I am proud of my slave heritage. (*Sings.*) We are survivors, I aint gon give in!!! We do what we got to do!

Dramatic
Lady Alice Augusta Granville Fossmire, late fifties

> *Lady Augusta is in her late fifties, the widowed moth-*
> *er of Detective Chief Inspector Gordon Fossmire. She*
> *is lecturing the members of a garden club about the*
> *mission of the Zero Population Party of Great Britain.*

LADY AUGUSTA: Ladies and gentlemen, we are a species
out of control. We are reproducing at alarming rates, and
our Earth Mother's milk of human kindness is turning
sour. In fact, she's poisoning us, especially in Cairo,
Calcutta, and Mexico City where the population's grown
so rampantly they can't control the sewage. There's
such high levels of fecal dust in the air that intestinal
parasites are infecting the tourists — not to mention the
natives. If you've read our pamphlet, you know one
out of seven of us lives on less than two dollars a day;
one out of three lacks modern sanitation; nearly eight
hundred million lack sufficient water; and eighteen thousand children under five die every day from preventable
causes. So how can we endure these calamities? The Zero
Population Party proposes universal vasectomies for all
adolescent males — after they preserve semen samples
for potential future families. This simple operation will
guarantee that no child is ever again born unwittingly or
unwanted. And it's high time for men to take the initia-
tive! For decades women have subjected their bodies to
chemicals that induce life threatening strokes, cancers
and bloatings so severe they inflate like balloons and fly
east — to China where they once wisely legislated one
child per family, only one. If we follow this dictum the
standard of living in the whole world will rise. If we
don't, Mother Earth will plague us with fires, floods,

famines, and national psychoses — with countries selling their excess into slavery or committing mass genocide. But what is genocide? A systematic solution? A war against humanity? An ugly little word? Or maybe it's a tea party. Oh, invitations have already been sent to the Jews, the Armenians, Albanians, Cambodians, Bosnians, and Tutsies. And where did they go? Down, down, down the rabbit hole to a tea party. Tea Party. Tea Party. Genocide. Genocide. It's all just words, you see, words, words, words!

For information on this author, click on the WRITERS tab at www.smithandkraus.com.

Dramatic
Johanna, late twenties

> *Turner Street's bold paintings are the hottest thing to hit*
> *the scene – they've even captured the attention of the*
> *elusive Johanna, a journalist posing as a cater-waitress*
> *to meet artists like Turner. Skipping out on the rest of*
> *the gallery opening festivities, Turner takes Johanna*
> *back to his loft, and what he thinks will be a night of*
> *romance goes awry when his one-eyed, pill-popping,*
> *younger brother Palmer shows up. In Johanna's attempt*
> *to get to the real truth behind Turner's art, she tells to*
> *Palmer that the paintings are of his missing eye. This*
> *throws Palmer into a frenzy in which he reveals that*
> *Johanna is a journalist, not after sex, but after a story.*
> *Turner sends Palmer out onto to balcony, and begs*
> *Johanna to leave him alone. He asks, why does it have*
> *to be about him? He suggests she write about another*
> *artist. This is her response.*

JOHANNA: He doesn't interest me. You interest me. *(Beat)*
When I'm interested in someone, it's passionate, it's
something burning under my skin, you know like the urge
that pushes you into your locked studio, the thing that
pushed you to paint— it's hot and violent and scary— Of
all people you should understand why the toothpick guy
doesn't urge me to sit down and write something. *(Beat)*
You'll be able to paint just fine. I've done this before. I've
taken an artist from—Look, call it crazy, but we do, you
and I, we do what we do for a reason. I want this story,
sure, but you need this story. More than anyone. You're
stuck. You're hiding behind Palmer— What you did to
him, the shame, the fear, the power of it. Yes! Power.

You are going to paint eye after eye after eye until you turn blue in the face, and by then no one is going to even remember your name. What I plan to do is prevent that. What I plan to do will open you up to your next level, to your next big thing, and the people who matter, the real people who matter, won't forget you. I don't expose to destroy, I expose to break you out. You need to break out. You don't want to go back to the life you've worked incredibly, and I mean incredibly, hard to bury. Do you?

(Beat.) I did my research, I dug deep enough— I found a picture of you, you must have been eighteen or twenty, standing next to a boy with an eye patch. I showed it to my editor, and suddenly you were much more than just some mysterious painter with a chip on his shoulder, and the more I dug up the more they wanted it. The more I wanted it. The real story behind the artist who quickly rose to fame. The mystery unwrapped. I know your dad was, he was no hero. Honorable discharge? I know about his DUI's, the cover-ups... And I know that he didn't die fire-fighting.

Dramatic
Johanna, late twenties

> *Turner Street's bold paintings are the hottest thing to hit
> the scene – they've even captured the attention of the
> elusive Johanna, a journalist posing as a cater-waitress
> to meet artists like Turner. Skipping out on the rest of
> the gallery opening festivities, Turner takes Johanna
> back to his loft, and what he thinks will be a night of
> romance goes awry when his one-eyed, pill-popping,
> younger brother Palmer shows up. After a night of
> exposed secrets and Cain and Abel-like fights between
> the brothers, which have been carefully orchestrated by
> Johanna, what she thought was controlled chaos finally
> goes too far, Palmer attempts suicide by drug overdose.
> This speech follows Turner's return from having just
> forced his brother to vomit. Turner exhausted sits on
> the couch drinking whiskey. Johanna, struggling with
> how far things have gotten, breaks the silence.*

JOHANNA: None of us deserve it. Having shit with our
parents. Things not being picture perfect, not the childhood of dreams. Not saying I had it as bad as you two,
not saying that at all... But mine wasn't Full House or
The Brady Bunch either. I think it rarely is, for anyone...
My mom, wow, she was this amazing person, kind, an
incredible baker, I mean her scones — She wanted to be
a... well she wanted to be an artist, she told me that once.
But she was stuck, she got really stuck, trapped under
this one thing that happened to her back in her not so
perfect childhood, I watched it change her. By the time I
was in middle school she barely left the house, she liked
to keep the curtains drawn. But still, she always smiled
like everything was perfect. Whatever it was, what she

held onto, held her back from even being just a mom sometimes, from being better... Sometimes I just wanted to break it out of her. Break her down. Let her let go. Let her just— Break. She left the world like a whimper. Never getting out of it, never getting on top of it. That's why I use her name. That's why doing this means something to me. Interests me. I've been able to break them. I thought I could... Palmer... I didn't know he would...

Seriocomic
Lucia, twenty-nine, Mexican American

> *Lucia, pronounced "Loo-chia," is a writer on a TV series. Here she tells her friend Abel, a janitor at the studio, about an incident that occurred in the writer's room.*

LUCIA: Oooh, Abel. You have to tell me if you know of a Señora that can do a *maleficio* on someone. I'll pay anything. I am seriously considering putting a hex on someone. "Witch" is offensive — I say Señora, but yes, I'm seriously in need of one — to fucking curse that Gary fucker who is the biggest hack who ever walked the fucking earth. OhmyGa. I can't fucking stand him. Look how late it is and we were all still up there because of him. He unravels the whole thing by pitching the most ridiculous thing in the history of things. He literally wants Rosa to frame someone by rubbing a dog — a DOG, Abel — on a bed. He's proposing she bring a little dog to this dirty cop's house and to literally RUB the little animal on a literal bed. And what's insane was that all the other writers were kind of nodding, not disagreeing, not saying "that is the most ridiculous thing on the planet" but just letting Gary talk. And I don't know when I dropped into my cunt but I said, "really? She's going to crawl in the window carrying a dog and then "rub" a bed with it?" And then it's like everyone woke up and John, sorry, my boss, snapped out of it... So, he — *mi "jefe"* — finally shuts that shit down. And this is when I see my chance, I guess, so I sit up and pitch, "why doesn't Rosa just leave dog hair on his clothes?" — I'll explain the whole thing. We have to link the dog to the guy. It's stupid. —Anyway. John was like, "oh, yeah. What a great idea, Lusha." That simple. And that was that. But Gary? He had daggers for me. I was like, I better wait down here in my office or he'll jump me in the parking lot.

Dramatic
Gloria, fifties

> *Gloria has been transported to a fantastical world after*
> *accidentally eating magic mushrooms. She reminisces*
> *about going to Carnival in Mexico City when she was*
> *young and in love.*

GLORIA: Is that cinnamon I taste? You know, the craziest thing happened? I was in the street, I was dancing and then I was swept up in a man's arms. He was wearing a crown, and then someone put a crown on me, or it just appeared suddenly, on my head and there was light coming from it, I suppose it had batteries of some kind. You have no idea of the power of those people, dancing and singing and it was religious in its nature. How do I know? Because of their faces, they were ecstatic, there is no other word for it, and I suppose I was, too, I certainly felt ecstatic. And then this man kissed me and we were spinning or we were standing still and the world was spinning and I closed my eyes and when I opened them, there was Julia. In my arms. I had been kissing her. I was a bit high. Everything kept changing. It was like I took a trip to the moon except instead of being barren the moon was full of life. Then I came home and married your father. He couldn't wait for me to finish school. I still have one more year and then I'd have my degree. Of course, I don't remember much of what I studied. I suppose Julia's married with a brood by now. She was very Mexican, you know. Catholic. Religious family, her brother was a priest. They had a husband picked out for her, what was his name, something, Fernando or Juan, I don't know, it doesn't matter. A big hulking figure. I remember he had hairy arms. And Julia was truly an aristocrat, spoke, I don't know, four or five languages, rode a horse like a general. One morning she woke me up just before dawn and insisted we go for a ride. Of course, Julia only rode bareback, have you ever tried it, the only way to stay on the horse is to hang on for dear life. You know, when you're moving fast like that, when it all depends on the powers of the earth and the sun and the sky and the beating heart of your companion, when you've had an experience like that, you never really get over it. Life goes on, you turn corner after corner, but the pulse of your life can never be the same when you have lived for a moment on the lip of eternity.

Seriocomic
Avery, early to mid-twenties

> *Avery is speaking to Max, her same age, a close friend*
> *from college, over the phone. Max's new girlfriend is*
> *moving in with him and Avery is worried it's too soon.*
> *She clearly harbors feelings for him, feelings she's had*
> *for years, and she's struggling to "approve" of this*
> *new relationship. At this point she hasn't directly told*
> *Max how she feels.*

AVERY: What? Holy shit, you've only known her like 3
months! ... No way. it's been like ... Well, still, you know,
it hasn't been that long, she must really ... Is your stupid
apartment big enough? We could barely fit that couch in
there when you moved in.

(in Max voice)

"PUSH THE STUPID THING FORWARD, AVE. *AVE.*
AVE." Well, congrats, Maxiepad. Yes, I will gladly warm
your house, Again. Yeah, who are Anna's friends, even?
I don't think I've ever ... [met any of her friends] Oh,
OK, sure, I'll just bring some girls for her to *know* in the
city. That's usually how it works, friendship. K, should
I be playing, like, the voice of reason here? ... *Because*,
because you sometimes do things on principle ... Um,
how 'bout everything you've ever *done*; your job, your
wrestling in college, working at Applebee's our senior
year ... Yeah, that's exactly the same thing! We'd all be
going out and you'd be like, "No, I have to work," and
we'd be all, "Why is Max working at Applebee's?" ...
I know, I can barely keep a fish alive, let alone a human
being ... But Max, you said all this stuff about Erin
don't forget, OK, you do things because you feel like

you *have* to, you get obsessed with an *idea* of … Shit, every time I'm on the F, I always— OK, can we finish this later, though? I think it's…Oh, shit. Yeah, I'm going in the tunnel.

For information on this author, click on the WRITERS tab at www.smithandkraus.com.

Seriocomic
Parker, twenty-seven

In the offices of the magazine Vanity Fair in the year 1920, Dorothy Parker is supposed to be training the young Edmund Wilson to replace her and Robert Benchley as assistant editors there. She is leaving in a dispute over her sometimes devastating but very funny theatre reviews, and her friend Benchley is leaving with her in protest. Parker and Benchley are part of the Algonquin Round Table, a group of writers who meet at the Hotel Algonquin, noted for their wicked sense of humor about others, each other, and themselves. She and Benchley call themselves Mrs. Parker and Mr Benchley and spend much of their time drinking when they're supposed to be working. Here she and Mr Benchley are having a very good time entertaining the young Wilson and his friend, the poet Edna Saint Vincent Millay, in an office that seems more like a circus.

PARKER: Actually, I am quitting, but it feels like being fired, and it's all Billie Burke's fault. Do you know Billie Burke? I wrote some rather nasty things about Billie Burke in one of my theatre reviews, which is one of the thoroughly disgusting and totally pointless jobs you're going to be stealing from us. I am a horrible woman. I take pride in it. But I'm a good writer. Whereas Billie Burke, on the other hand, is a horrible actress. At least in her current unfortunate theatrical manifestation. She might be quite a wonderful actress in some other manifestation at some later date. And if so, I'll be more than happy to say so. But in this one, she's really stinking up 42nd Street. Which didn't smell all that good to begin with. Unfortunately, Billie Burke is sleeping with Flo Ziegfeld. And Flo Ziegfeld is a good friend of Condé Nast. And Condé Nast owns *Vanity Fair*. So when Mr Ziegfeld read that I said Billie Burke had all the onstage charisma of a can of oysters, he was understandably upset. So he called up Condé Nast. And when Condé Nast, who is a pompous dickhead, told Mr Crowninshield that I must under no circumstances ever be allowed to compare Billie Burke to a can of oysters, I protested that I'm a theatre critic, and it's my job to say horrible things about people. So Mr Crowninshield told me I couldn't write any more theatre reviews, and I told him in that case I'd have no choice but to resign in protest. It's not that I enjoy saying horrible things about people ... All right, I do enjoy saying horrible things about people. But only if they're funny. I suppose I really am a horrible person. But that's why you love me. Mr Benchley really does love me. Which is why he very gallantly also resigned. And Bob Sherwood, in support of both of us, also resigned. It was the worst massacre since General Custer met Crazy Horse. Do you know Bob Sherwood? The playwright. It's actually rather confusing. Robert Benchley. Robert E. Sherwood. Sherwood Anderson. Maxwell Anderson. Elsa Maxwell. Nobody can keep them straight. They're all pretty much the same person. But Mr Benchley and I agreed to stay on long enough to train you. Purely out of the goodness of our hearts. And because we need the money. Mr Benchley and I have no money. We're writers. So, here's how things work here at *Vanity Fair*. Over there, you can see a pile of unsolicited manuscripts, roughly the size of Mount Kilimanjaro. As these unsolicited manuscripts come in, you need to carefully log in this record book the title of the piece, the name of the author, and the date received. Do you follow me so far? Mr Benchley often follows me in the street. He drinks all day at work and then gets lost on the way home. I try to lose him but often I fail. It's like being stalked by a stray dog. Anyway, once you've carefully written down all that information, you take the manuscript, go over to the window, and throw it out, like this.

(She hurls a manuscript out the window.)

You see? It's all in the wrist.

THE GODDESS OF MURDEROUS RAIN

Don Nigro

Dramatic
Millay, Twenty-nine

> *Edna Saint Vincent Millay, already a famous poet in her twenties, is just back from a long trip to Europe, and runs into her old friend Edmund (Bunny) Wilson, who is deeply in love with her, at a party in Greenwich Village, where she is a legendary for her uninhibited sexual exploits and mysterious fairy girl charm. For some years she has been quite happily promiscuous, pursued by many, caught by quite a few, but never allowing herself to be trapped in a relationship. But now, having returned from a rather harrowing time in Europe, which she describes here to Wilson, her wild life is starting to catch up with her, and she is grow-ing tired of breaking hearts and raising havoc. They are walking on MacDougal street at night. The year is 1922 or so.)*

MILLAY: I'm completely miserable. I can't seem to get close enough to things. And when I do, I panic and run away. I thought Europe would cheer me up, but travel just makes you more lonely. There was an Englishman and then another one and then I went to Albania and made love in a tent and then back to Paris where I had a brief affair with a very nice woman and then I met a Frenchman, which is often the beginning of a sad story, a loathsome, fish faced, oily, boneless, sucker mouthed parasite, so of course I couldn't resist him. He put a child in me. Then he slithered away, leaving a trail of slime behind him. Mother would have killed him if there'd been an ax handy. She took me to the country. Studied old herbals. Found what she needed in the woods. Gave it to me in strong tea. And blood flowed again. The ritual sacrifice had been performed. How could you give yourself to that horrible man? she asked me. I don't know, I said. It was like I had no choice. He looked like your father, she said. And she was right. Then, on the ship coming home, I was seasick, and the orchestra kept playing "Ain't We Got Fun." I've never in my life come so close to going on a berserk murder spree in the horn section. What's it called when you slaughter an entire musical ensemble? Orchestricide? Then today I was staring into a marble table top and saw a face looking back at me which I was convinced was the Prince of Darkness, come to take my soul. Tramping around Albania like Lord Byron and having somebody lick pomegranate juice off your breasts while wolves howl in the ravine is all rather exciting, but then you're home again and what have you got? A few blurred photographs and saddle sores on your ass. And all the people you thought you loved blend together in your head. You might as well have imagined it all.

Don Nigro

Dramatic
Millay, fifty-six

> *Once the most desired and sexually active fairy girl*
> *and goddess in Greenwich Village, the poet Edna Saint*
> *Vincent Millay is now 56, prematurely old, worn out*
> *from all her adventures, long isolated in her upstate*
> *home, addicted to alcohol and morphine, and worried*
> *that her poetry has not been good enough and her life*
> *wasted. Her great friend Bunny, now the critic Edmund*
> *Wilson, once deeply in love with her, has come to visit*
> *after a 19 year estrangement, and here she tries to make*
> *sense of her life, and figure out where it's gone wrong.*

MILLAY: How to succeed in poe-biz: write a good poem.
Send them your photograph, imply that you might sleep
with them. Pretend to faint. Sleep with them. You can't
possibly understand, when you're young, how quickly
it can disappear. One minute so many people are in love
with you they're crawling over the corpses of past lovers
to get to you. The next morning you look in the mirror and
see nobody looking back at you. The writing is flowing so
beautifully you're convinced it will never stop, then one
day you open the door in your head and there's nobody
home. And all those who once trembled breathlessly for
your next word can't remember your name. We've come
a long way from that apartment you had in the Village
that smelled of wet cats, where I used to come and take
baths. Or was that Johnny? Oh, you're still bitter. That's
rather gratifying. Observe the beautiful fairy girl in her
wreckage. I could get away with absolutely anything. I
tried to get kicked out of Vassar, but they always forgave
me. I had the power to make anybody fall in love with
me. Men, women, children, animals. I could make plants

fall in love with me. And once I realized I could do it, I couldn't seem to stop. It's not that I didn't feel things. It's that I felt every single thing it's possible to feel. I suck up pain like a sponge. Things that happened forty years ago hurt just as much now. When I was a girl, I performed arcane ceremonies with candles to summon my father's ghost. And he wasn't even dead. I've spent my life looking for that ghost. Certain men have served as incarnations. Something in their eyes. Then the enchantment fades. When he was dying, I took care of him. But all love comes too late. Don't fuss over me, he said. Just play cards. For money. Pennies are fine. But he cheated. My father cheated me over pennies on his deathbed. He couldn't help it. He was bitten by a rabid Queen of Spades. He had the bluest eyes. I was fornicating with his doctor's daughter. Then he ruined everything by getting well, and I left and broke the doctor's daughter's heart, and so, to comfort her, my father slept with her. And I looked in the mirror and realized we're just alike, my father and I. Bunny, what happened to us?

Seriocomic
Franny, thirties

> *Franny is Addressing the audience. She and her hus-*
> *band Ray have been struggling to get pregnant, and*
> *dissatisfied by the medical options available. Franny*
> *meets Andy, and realizes he is the donor for her—but*
> *she hasn't broken the news yet to Ray. Franny attempts*
> *to explain her impulsive behavior.*

FRANNY: I travel on instinct. I'll try to explain. There are always conflicting paths in life, right? Your mother wants you to be a teacher, your father wants you to be an… astrophysicist. And you? Who knows what you want? So to the normal person, you have choice A and you have choice B.Or, choice C, which is 'none of the above,' or choice D which is something else entirely—but whatever; it's an imperfect metaphor. Some people decide based on logic. For some, it's financial, spiritual, emotional, whatever. I have to feel my way through. Ever since I was little, there has always been something in me that just… feels right about one way or the other. I can't explain it beyond that. It's like, instinct. That's how I found Ray. I was dating some guy named Pete in undergrad—some pseudo intellectual who was obsessed with action movies and chaos theory—not necessarily in that order—but I was out with Pete one night, in this seedy stockbroker bar in lower Manhattan. Pete goes to the bathroom, and some other guy makes a beeline for my table, sits down, and starts to chat me up about, I don't know, politics or religion or something useless. Before we get any further: that other guy wasn't Ray. Ray was that other guy's friend. At the bar, kinda cute, but totally embarrassed at his buddy's lack of tact. Anyway,Pete comes back and I can tell; there is this awkward uber-masculine alpha male bullshit that's about to go down at my table. But suddenly, I get a sense—an urge—it's almost uncanny, like my subconscious has figured out something that comes from outer space. I excuse myself from the testosterone-fest, walk right up to Ray, and put my arm in his. I tell him, "I'm going to take you out on a date. And before the end of tonight, you're going to want to marry me." He said: "Can I sleep with you first?" And I said, "You better." And I was right. Trusting my instincts.

Dramatic
Franny, thirties, to the audience.

> *Franny, without consulting her husband Ray, has implied that Andy, their sperm donor, might have a relationship with their future child. When Ray ends their relationship with Andy in anger, Franny is afraid her actions have caused irreparable damage to her marriage.*

FRANNIE: When I was thirteen, I wrote a list of the different qualities I wanted in a husband. It was written on the inside back cover of a notebook — although I don't remember which subject —it would be great if it were science, but that's conjecture. I'm sure it was surrounded by hearts and rainbows and block letters reading "Franny loves" some random boy. But I was so mad at Ray after the dinner, and the list, clear as day, popped into my mind.

It said:

My husband needs to be handsome.
He needs to be smart.
He needs to be nice;
he needs to be clean.
He needs to be strong enough to carry me when I'm too tired to walk.
He needs to be rich enough to buy me what I want, when I want it.
He needs to be willing to jump off a really high wall if I ask him.
He needs to love animals. Except spiders. He can hate spiders.
He needs to be able to make me laugh.

It was a fantasy—it was a dream list. Probably similar

to every other girl in school. We all had lists; we were thirteen and bored. That's what you do when you can't smoke or drink or see R rated movies. But twenty years later, I remember this list so well.

And Ray? He has so many of these qualities. How was I able to find someone to come so close to that pre-adolescent, absurdly hormonal, completely unrealistic wish list? But I did. And the most important, saved for last… he needs to make me laugh. Even when the jokes are predictable. Even when it's the same story I've already heard. It's one of the reasons I married him. That, and the fact that I am impulsive and a little reckless, and he is … neither of those things. But this… there's nothing funny about this. And part of me wants to hear him make some clever quip to put us at ease, make us forget —so we could at least get back to where we were before. I desperately need... to get back to where we were before.

Comic
Sister Yolanda, mid-forties

> *Sister Yolanda, a somewhat eccentric nun in her*
> *mid-forties (age is optional) is explaining to Phil*
> *Crane, an unhappy, divorced man in his late for-*
> *ties, whom she earlier physically assaulted, why his*
> *life will turn around if he will begin to live a more*
> *spiritual existence in a monastery with a bunch of*
> *monks.*

SISTER YOLANDA: Look, as I tried to explain to you all, this is my first big assignment from our Cherished Deity, the first time he's ever wanted me to get involved in something special and it's obvious like everything else in my life, I'm screwing it up. You are obviously a man who has lost his way, Mr. Crane. I would like to put you on the right path. I made a sacred vow to bring you back to the flock. We are all members of the flock, Mr. Crane. Unfortunately, some members seem to have flown off in the wrong direction. It's all so obvious now what I need to do. If I can change the direction of one human being, that one human being being you, lead him back to a life of love and peace, bring a tranquility to his existence that is obviously missing, then my life will finally matter and not be the pile of shit that at the present, both our lives seem to be. And to finally bring calm and quiet to a soul in obvious torment. It's not the convent you'll be going to. We share the property with a bunch of monks who live in a monastery about half a mile away. The Brotherhood of the Soil. A wonderful group of men dedicated to honoring and preserving life at its basic core. They don't believe in inside plumbing. I promise you, Mr. Crane, you will find the tranquility that is now missing in your life.

For information on this author, click on the WRITERS tab at www.smithandkraus.com.

Comic
Sister Yolanda, mid-forties

> *Sister Yolanda, a somewhat eccentric nun, is explaining
> to a group of people in a New York apartment why she
> is there and why she physically attacked Phil Crane,
> the unhappy, divorced man who resides there.*

SISTER YOLANDA: Please forgive me. I'm just a little more on
edge than usual because this undertaking is so important to
me. You see up until Mr. Crane's letter I found myself floun-
dering again. Outside of the usual routines at the convent,
prayer, reflection, meditation, gluing labels on jelly jars, I
still felt unfulfilled, empty, living a life without purpose, I
began to feel God was ignoring me again, avoiding me. But
then your letter showed up and it all turned around for me.
I don't know why but I found myself reading it over and
over and over and then about the tenth or eleventh time, out
of the blue I began to hear this glorious music along with a
soft, angelic chorus of Hallelujahs...

(Begins singing.)

Hallelujah! Hallelujah! Hal-el-lu-jah... backed up by this
magnificent stringed ensemble playing the most beautiful
rendition of "Ave Maria" imaginable.

*(Begins humming "Ave Maria" interrupting the hum-
ming with Hallelujahs. Her eyes are closed in rapture.)*

It grew louder and louder. And then, above it all came this
majestic, imposing voice, booming to me "It's your turn girl!
Go after it and kick ass! And there it was. I had just received
my first mission from our Divine Commander. Yes! Yes! Yes!

For information on this author, click on the
WRITERS tab at www.smithandkraus.com.

THE GRASS IS GREENEST AT THE HOUSTON ASTRODOME.

Michael Ross Albert

Dramatic
Amy, late twenties-early thirties

> *After a jealous painter destroys her colleagues' artwork in a fit of rage, Amy, the manager of a floundering independent art gallery confronts her friends.*

AMY: Do you mind if... Do you mind if everyone just left? Would that be something you could all do right now? The art gallery that I manage is in disarray. Each of you is my friend, though sometimes I have no idea why or if that's even true, but the fact remains that your work would not have been represented on these walls tonight, or in any group show we've ever hosted, had it not been for my involvement in the curation process. And instead of saying, "Thank you, Amy, how nice that was of you." Or, "Gee, Amy, this sure was a swell opening, sorry the gallery's closing, thanks for the free wine and the hors d'oeuvres, and the exposure in this whatever storefront art gallery, I'm really happy to have been a part of it." Instead of showing even a hint of gratitude, even the slightest bit of thanks for the effort I put into tonight's event, this one is so petty that she literally tears other artists' paintings off the walls — and all because someone bought Marshall's green thing and not your vaginal thing, whatever the hell it is. I am having a nightmare of an evening, if you haven't noticed. If it hadn't occurred to you yet. I had to convince the police to keep from sending you to a mental hospital, Caroline. Do you understand me? A mental hospital. With padded walls and straight-jackets. And maybe I don't want to hear your snide remarks either, Pablo. Maybe I'm a little tired. And a little frustrated. And maybe I need to sweep some fucking glass off the fucking floor. So maybe you should all just get the fuck out of my gallery before I take this broom and shove it up each of your assholes. Okay?

Dramatic
Angela, thirty-three, Latina.

> *Angela's husband Ramiro is a drone pilot who was*
> *involved in a friendly-fire incident that killed a number*
> *of U.S. soldiers. She addresses Shanti, a woman who*
> *was once named Cheryl. They meet in a place that only*
> *exists between them.*

ANGELA: I didn't say some of that——the last part. He didn't say that either. In fact, he didn't say anything. People try to pull bullets out of their own skulls. People try to push the train off just as they've shoved themselves underneath. People, in all their beautiful and convoluted complications will try to save themselves even when they are hell bent on their desire to die. He had hope for humankind. Human-mean. Human beings. He, my beautiful husband, had hope. And we shouldn't give sordid jobs like that to the hopers. We should save those jobs for the cynics of the world. People who divorce soul from action. People like me. Reality is, hopers and truth-tellers often fall in love. The secret about hopers is that deep down they are depressed, and they've just awashed themselves in hope, like it's some kind of magical sealant. *(ironically)* Hopers. Truth-tellers are from a different planet entirely. They're from another galaxy. They reel their truths, like vomit, and expect the places and the people that they land upon, just to take it. Because it's the truth. And the truth matters. *(And then)* What kind are you, Cheryl?

Comic

Renee, twenties

> *Poor Renee Purdy. It's her best friend Francie's wed-*
> *ding day, and Francie's gone and barricaded herself*
> *up in the church nursery and is refusing to come down*
> *and get married. Not that Maid of Honor Renee isn't*
> *having problems of her own. While things remain up in*
> *the air, twenty-something Renee has slipped out of the*
> *church to check on her grandmother and now returns*
> *to unload on the wedding's caterer, Ms. Rosenhaus.*
> *Poor Ms. Rosenhaus.*

RENEE: My car broke down. I had only driven two short
blocks, and it just up and died. I was on my way to check
on my grandmother. She broke her hip last week. She was
in one of those mechanical chairs that lifts you to your
feet from a seated position. Well, the chair went haywire
while she was watching an old *Cheers* episode last Sat-
urday night and pitched her right across the room. We're
suing, of course, but only for medical expenses. Granner
doesn't believe in punitive remuneration. *(Pause)* This
has not been a good week for me. First, Granner gets
thrown through the air like a discarded puppet, then Francie decides at the very last minute that she doesn't want
to marry Kyle. And now my car is dead, and I don't know
a single mechanic who isn't going to charge me an arm
and a leg to get it fixed, plus I left my "something blue"
for Francie back at my apartment, not that she needs it
now anyway. And would you look at this?

(She opens her mouth wide.)

I have a canker inside my mouth which came like a thief

in the night and which is making me want to scream. Anyway, my luck is about to change. This is what Vivinette says. She does my charts. My star charts. Vivinette says I'm about to meet someone who will change my life forever. In a positive way. In a very positive, yet earth-shattering way.

Comic
Francie, twenties

> *Twenty-something Francie Renfro is having second thoughts about marrying Kyle Longacre. On their wedding day. It's because there's another man she's fallen in love with—Gert Fleers. Gert, as she explains to befuddled members of the wedding party, is the real man of her dreams. Her sleeping prince. Well, to be accurate: her comatose prince.*

FRANCIE: I've wanted to. So badly. I know it sounds weird, but it's all I've been thinking about lately. That this *is* a beautiful fairy tale, and that it's going to have a fairy tale ending! And last week I came so very close to doing it — to actually kissing him. I was inches from his lips. My heart was racing. I was so scared. There I was: poised and ready — just waiting for the courage to come and propel my lips toward his. Then the nurse walked in.

> *(in the urse's voice)*

"What on Earth are you doing, young lady? Get down off that patient!"

> *(turning to her own voice)*

It was then that I realized I'd climbed right up into bed with him and was at that moment kind of straddling him like the way that wrestlers sometimes pin each other down. I was so mortified. I fled from that hospital room in shame, and tried not to think of kissing him that way again. But I think about it all the time. But this time he's kissing me and I'm kissing him right back.

Comic
Renee, twenties

> *Renee Purdy, Maid of Honor to her best friend Francie*
> *Renfro, returns to the church, where Francie's wedding*
> *remains on hold, because Francie has decided to give*
> *her heart to another man. The other man is Gert Fleers,*
> *who has just come out of his month-long coma, only*
> *to be displaced from his hospital bed by an accident*
> *that has befallen the visiting president of the United*
> *States. It is Renee who actually kissed Francie's sleep-*
> *ing prince and brought him to consciousness, only to*
> *discover that the man with whom she was also falling*
> *in love is a man she no longer wants anything to do*
> *with. She explains to the other members of the wedding*
> *party all that has transpired ... while picking chicken*
> *feathers out of her hair.*

RENEE: Then I guess you don't know what happened to the
President. The motorcade was headed back to the airport,
and just as the presidential limousine turns the corner
onto Adams, it has to make this sudden swerve to miss
this — this *basketball* that's just sitting right there in the
middle of their lane... and the limo goes out of control
and sideswipes this row of parked cars, and then it jumps
the curb and nearly runs over this group of sweet little
kindergarten children waving their miniature American
flags, and then it plows right into that awful statue in
front of the municipal library — you know, the one of
the pioneer woman churning butter. And so the Pioneer
Lady topples off her pedestal and onto the top of the
limo, and her butter churn breaks in two and the handle
goes through the sunroof of the limo and knocks the
President in the head, and they have to rush him straight

to Mercy Presbyterian. His press secretary says he has a knot on his head the size of a tangerine. That's not all. They decide to put him in Gert's wing. On Gert's floor. So the Secret Service men, they make the hospital staff clear out all the patients on that floor — you know, for security reasons — but it's not done in a very organized fashion. There was this terrible head-on gurney collision. Anyway, I end up in the parking lot, and suddenly I see Gert waving at me from a window on the second floor. I go over to him. And we look at each other, you know: lovingly, for a moment, and the late afternoon sun is catching the blond highlights in his soft brown hair. And his sky-blue eyes are dancing and sparkling, and his smile is sending me to some far away exotic place, and then he opens his mouth — finally — to speak. It's the ugliest, foulest-sounding croak I've ever heard in my life. Like he was gargling rocks or something. That horrible voice — it sends a shiver through my body. And all the love I had for him — it just — it just dribbles away. So I run. I run all the way to Fillmore and hitch a ride with the first car — well, it's actually a truck. It's a chicken farmer who brings me right over. So I can apologize to Francie for kissing her dream man and waking him up. And so I can warn her.

Seriocomic
Sunshine, 25-35

*Setting: The office of "Hired Expectations" Employ-
ment Agency—little more than a make-shift rented
closet off the lobby of a Chinese take-out. Sunshine,
the "owner" and only employee, is anxious to retain
her only walk-in customer of the day, Dudley, an un-
employed skywriting pilot, who has grown suspicious
of her operation.*

SUNSHINE: Stop, Mister D, please! Please! Please. It's been
a rough year for me, too. Until recently, I too was flying
high. I had a six-figure income on the sixteenth floor of
a sixty-six-story corporate monolith. Life was sweet.
Then, my dream world came crashing down. The virtual
company I had telemarketed for for four years virtually
disappeared overnight. Samantha is not my secretary;
she's my German Shepherd—who I can barely keep in
kibble since that fateful day when my world was shaken.
On my way home from the worst day of my professional
career—do you know how despairing it is to be rejected
for a *telemarketing* job?— my timing belt broke. Leaving
me stranded in the parking lot of the 7-11 next door. I
looked at the clock: it was exactly 7:11 p.m. A cruel joke
of the universe or a twist of fate? Glass half-empty, glass
half full, Mister D? As I waited for triple-A to arrive,
contemplating moving Samantha and me into a double-
wide Frigidaire box under the freeway overpass, I felt
a sensation right here in the pit of my stomach. Call it
intuition. Call it a higher calling. Call it hunger pangs—
since I had skipped lunch and found myself enveloped by
a spicy cloud of Kung Pao Shrimp… But it was a sign,

Mister D, a sign—just like you said. A sign! that flashed, "Happy Lucky Panda Chinese Food and Donut." That sign saved me and Samantha from a life of corrugated contumely. It flashed to me a sort of neon morse code, this simple truth: If those who cannot do, teach; and those who cannot play, coach; then, those who cannot find work, should work in Human Resources! The next day I took every single penny I had salted away in my TIAA-Cref account and sunk it into this business. And I have never looked back—not once. And that was almost (checks her watch) forty-seven hours ago. Here I am, Mister D: a survivor—just like you. (Pounding her desk to emphasize each word) A. Survivor. Who. Is. Asking. For. A. Chance. A chance from another survivor who knows what it means to survive. Who knows how a little faith can move a mountain, form an LLC, and get a once-grounded pilot into the sky again. Are ye a man of faith, Mister D? Then, I ask you to give me that chance. I ask you to have faith in your faith in me. For your sake, for my sake, and for the sake of a German Shepherd whose belief in me has been heretofore unshaken. I want to be the entrepreneur my dog expects me to be. I want to be the headhunter *you* expect me to be. I will find you the job! I will give you the chance to slip the surly bonds and stroke yourself against God's face! All I need is your approval. And your word. And 20% commission for the next three years. Do we have a deal?

For information on this author, click on the WRITERS tab at www.smithandkraus.com.

Libby Emmons

Seriocomic
Ames, twenties

> *Ames is going through an existential crisis about her
> identity and her future. She's speaking to the audience.*

AMES: I'm a white woman being written about by a white
woman. I don't feel weird about it except that I feel
weird about everything. I get this feeling, like deep down
inside myself, that I am boring. I think about my mom,
and how she was nice to me, and made me cheese and
apple sandwiches with honey when I went on field trips,
and always left a little note in my back pack when I would
go to visit my dad, and I would find it when I unpacked
and it always made me cry. And that is boring. And I
think about my cousins in Maine and how pretty their
little children are when the sun glints off of their hair.
And that is boring. And my father is boring, even how
he threatened to beat up my boyfriend one time it was
predictable. Now my fate is to be a boring white woman
being written about by a boring white woman. And the
fact that we feel deeply is irrelevant because everyone
feels deeply. There is no end to how deeply everyone can
feel, it's the same as how everyone eats. What if I just
love someone and want to have babies? Does that make
me a bad feminist? When I finished graduate school I was
lucky that I already had a job at the café, even though I
hate the café. My Gramma says "honey, be grateful." But
then she tells me all the ways I should do better. I don't
like feeling like I'm meaningless. But of course no one
wants to feel that way, so even at my most miserable I'm
exactly the same as everyone else.

Dramatic
Danesha, twenties/thirties, African American

*Danesha is in her late 20's/early 30's, Danesha was
working on a career as a professional dancer before she
moved back home and opened her own dance studio.
She's speaking to the audience.*

DANESHA: I went to school to be a dancer. I studied all the
greats. I worked on my body. I imbibed hallucinogenic
drugs in an effort to open my mind to new ideas, new
ways of moving through space, new ways of manipulat-
ing the matter that is my body. I had this idea that everything I was doing to myself, for myself, had meaning.
I went into debt with faith in my meaning. I did all the
things a girl with talent and brains and drive is supposed
to do. I sacrificed relationships in favor of my career. I
moved to New York and auditioned for everything, had
drinks with anyone who might have a lead on a solid
gig. I worked my ass off for free. These are the things
we do, we women with talent and ambition, we put it
all on the line week after week, month after month, year
after year. I did that. I hustled. Until one day there was
no hustle left. I was done. I moved home. I started giving
dance lessons. At the end of the year I rent a big hall for
the recitals. The little kids like it best, twirling around in
silly costumes while their parents take movies and brag
about how their little kid is the best one, or the worst one,
or the one with the best balance, or the one with the most
heart. It doesn't matter what it is but these parents out
here take pride in it, same as mine did. I want to warn
them, these kids, to not look at life with such big eyes. In
life there's no such thing as a Participation Trophy. But
instead I- I give them all ribbons, pin them to their little

costumes, and bring in cupcakes and juice to celebrate. I see these big eyes.

Dramatic
Arella, thirties, Native American

> *Arella is a member of an isolated Native American tribe, which suffers from a devastatingly high rate of diabetes. Jillian, a genetic anthropologist would like to collect blood from the tribe to see if there's a genetic component to their diabetes, but the tribe has never given blood before – they believe their blood is sacred. Arella tries to explain her tribe's perspective to Jillian, who is somewhat tone-deaf to their concerns.*

ARELLA: *(furious)* Classes in nutrition. You think we want to be eating that garbage? You think we wouldn't rather be hunting and farming our own food like we did for a thousand years? On our own land? Seven million acres was our territory. Seven *million.* All of Cataract Canyon. Until you cut us down to nothing. Put restrictions on our water access. How could we farm? During dry times, the cattle died. The crops died. By the time we got back a few thousand acres — and we had to fight for decades to get them back — we hadn't farmed for generations. We'd become dependent on tourism. What else could we do? You took away our livelihood, and now you mock us for eating the garbage you ship in. "You really believe that?" That's what you said. "You really believe that?" As if we're stupid. Ignorant. I'm so tired of you deciding, if we don't believe what you believe, we're primitive. Uneducated. We have "myths" and you have "truth." Your truth. You know, there's always a new truth. The latest scientific breakthrough. The new discovery. And then a few years later, it's disproven, and there's a newer truth. Well, we've believed what we believe for a thousand years, and it's sustained us through some very bad times. So, don't come here. To my home. And say to me "you really believe that? You really teach your children that?" We teach our children generosity and respect. Honor the elders. Keep our traditions alive. Because this is our heritage. This is our life. Stop taking and taking and taking away our life.

For information on this author, click on the WRITERS tab at www.smithandkraus.com.

Dramatic
Louise, fifty to late sixties

> *After serving seven years in prison, Louise returns to California's Inland Empire and her family's home, a dilapidated horse ranch that is being used as a front to run drugs. She explains to her daughter Jolie Beth why years ago, she stole her first lover, and why she converted from the Christian faith to Islam while in prison.*

LOUISE: There's this thing inside of me, it's a competition that I don't want anyone else to win. Don't care what it is, if I see someone doing better than me, I don't want them to and I have to stop them. I cannot watch someone being happy when I'm miserable, rich when I'm poor, in love when I'm alone. That's something that's inside of me and in prison I learned to push it down and keep it down. Eventually I learned to... just get rid of it. Do you know what the state's idea of drug rehabilitation is? They throw you in a cell with three other women. They don't give you any drugs. They give you nothing and leave you in there to detox. There's no substances to substitute. Your body attacks you. Your brain starts to overload. You need something, anything, to feed the monster inside you. You scream and sweat and yell and puke and if you're lucky, someone in your cell understands and they clean you up and give you sips of water. It feels like fire. A burning, white, hot fire inside your chest. You scream and cry, trying to put the fire out, but all you're really doing is rolling around on the floor in your own filth. They stuck me in a cell with three of the baddest black Muslim women in the place, thinking they'd beat my ass cause I was white... but those ladies knew what I was going through, two of them had been through it themselves, and they took care of me and when I came out of it they taught me. They taught me a lot of things. It might come back. I could revert back to what I used to be and turn into the old Louise, but I'm trying... I'm trying so hard not to and I hold on to all their lessons, just fighting to try to hear those women's voices that taught me, "If you forgive, You are the Almighty, the All-Wise."

Dramatic
Louise, fifty to late sixties

> *After serving seven years in prison, Louise returns to California's Inland Empire and her family's home, a dilapidated horse ranch that is being used as a front to run drugs She tells her sister June and her daughter Jolie Beth that she gave her oldest daughter her first shot of heroin many years ago, and explains how she learned what forgiveness was really about while serving time in prison.*

LOUISE: You want to hate me for it. Go ahead. I'm doing what I can now to fix things. I'm trying to fix it... but yeah, it's true... and.... Oh God...

(She collapses to the floor like she wants to pray and at the same time, tries to hold herself together as she rips off the taqiyah - a Muslim prayer cap - that she is wearing.)

The man that gave me this hat, he taught me a lot of things. He could see the pain in my eyes, on my face. They'd let him come into the prison once a week and talk to us. He was an *Iman*, a leader and a teacher. A really nice man. I learned what I could from this good man, he even gave me his own personal copy of the Quran. He had hand written notes in it and passages marked, but the first thing I read, the very first thing he told me to read, was a passage I memorized. "Do not ask about matters which, if they were made known to you, would make things difficult for you. If you do ask about them when the Quran is being set down, they will be made known to you. Allah has ignored them. Allah is Ever- Forgiving, All-Forbearing." You don't want to forgive me? You don't want to make a new life and include me in it? That's okay. I need somebody in my life that is all forgiving, who ignores my short comings. If it can't be my family and God, then it will just have to be God... because he forgives me, even when no one else will.

Comic
Lorrie, thirty

Lorrie is addressing a female director about her encounter with David Mamet at a rehearsal for a revival of Glengarry Glen Ross.

LORRIE: David Mamet would have none of it, although it would have been a tremendous improvement on *Glengarry Glen Ross*. But he wouldn't listen. Whoever heard of a play that didn't have at least one female character? I'll tell you what play, his! You know what his problem is? He has his own personal war on women, actresses in particular. His play has zero, nada, not one feminine soul. I wouldn't be in his play now even if he begged me. After all, I literally handed him the female character, an Indian to boot, a Mrs. Patel, who is only briefly mentioned in *Glengarry Glen Ross*, doesn't even play a pivotal role. I wrote the dialogue, inserted the scenes where she appears, and she's pissed, a cat on a hot tin roof kind of woman, who doesn't like to be taken advantage of, a three-dimensional character who takes all of those salesmen to the wall for all their thieving and lying because of their unbridled capitalism gone amok. I'm not a socialist, mind you, but I believe in fair play, where everyone has a chance to succeed in this hollowed out middle class kind of world. I may be just a saleswoman, but I don't shilly shally and take advantage of women looking to spritz some perfume on their bodies to get their men folk juiced up so they can get a little loving. Hell, I barely make more than minimum wage at Macy's, and of course I have to participate in that freakin' sham of a turkey day parade with all those bloated cartoon characters. I don't even like turkey. It's a fucking ugly bird.

I'm a halibut, haddock kind of woman. I hardly ever eat meat, but David Mamet is a meat eater if ever I saw one, believe you me. He's got incisors you wouldn't believe. Big mother fucking teeth to gnaw at your bones, deep into your marrow. What the fuck! He wouldn't even listen to my argument. But you, at least, gave me the courtesy to hear me out, to present my case, but that's because you're a woman who understands what we're up against, and that's what I really like about you, because not all women are like you. Band of brothers? We need a band of sisters! You'd think we'd all stick together and give it to the man, that's right the MAN, who wants to ultra sound us to death, monitor our vaginas, clamp down on our clitoris except where it suits him, and ultimately take us back to the stone age of Neanderthal hubba hubba. Well, fuck that! It's Alamo time for women in the theater business, in all businesses, in all walks of life, and I'm leading the fucking charge! Do I sound like a fucking feminist? No! Just one pissed off lady.

For information on this author, click on the WRITERS tab at www.smithandkraus.com.

Seriocomic
January, twenties to forties

> *January is an unkempt woman in a prison interroga-*
> *tion room.*

JANUARY: I didn't kill him. I know that's what you're thinkin', but I didn't. I came in there and I found him. There. Like that. All bloody in the face and all? And… and all I wanted to do was see my son. But that son-of-a bitch wouldn't let me. I'm sorry. E'scuse my French. He's not a son-of-a-bitch, his mammy was religious. Or… so he says. But oooh, he make me mad. For four years, you… You know, f' four years, we was together, before we had Allegro? Four years. I damn near went crazy waitin' for that man to innaduce me to his family. But he never did. He kept sayin I was trashy. Was no good for his mom and dad to meet me. Of course, he didn't tell me none of that when I was kissing on his penis, though, I'll tell you that much. I wasn't too trashy f' him to fuck me, but when it came time f' family, it was… I'm sorry. E'scuse my French. *(Beat)* Fuck that, I hope he *is* in hell. Did you know he was a vegetarian? And all he ever ate was cauliflower. Not even collard greens. Just cauliflower, celery, and broccoli. And this Japanese fotu stuff. It was nasty. I kept telling him it wasn't Christian. God made animals for our consumption, right? But he believed in God, and I… guess he knew what he was sayin'. I just… I don't know. It don't seem right to me. If God don't want us eatin' animals, then why the hell he make 'em out of *meat*? But I guess he didn't learn the same things in his Sunday school like I learned in mine. I don't know. When Allegro was born, you see… Charles kep' sayin we wasn't gonna' feed him no meat or nothin.

We was gonna feed him bean sprouts. Frankly, and I'm a' you the God's honest truth right now – I'm glad he's dead. I ain't gonna' lie to you. That son-of… That *man*. What kind of man don't feed his son no hamburgers? No bar-b-que? They's something wrong with that.

Arlene Hutton

Dramatic
Katelyn, seventeen

Katelyn, a high school junior, tells the audience about the time her dance partner felt her up.

KATELYN: So I dance, right? Since I was like six. Tutus, recitals, the whole thing. And I go to these big dance conferences. A bunch of us from the dance studio go. With our teachers. And we take these classes taught by professional dancers. From like New York. So I'm in this pas de deux class at the conference—we don't have pas deux at my studio because there aren't any boys—but at the conference I'm in this class. And this guy I just met is my partner. He's all sweaty from another class right before, but, well, that's something you have to get over when you're a dancer like I am. We start off with some simple lifts, like his hands are at my waist and he holds me up when I jump and it's really cool. It's like flying and I'm jumping higher than I ever have before. And then the teacher shows us some harder lifts and she demonstrates and we mark them. "Marking" is what you do when you aren't dancing full out. So we "mark" this move where he lifts me one way and then turns me and I slide down. It's okay. And then we try it for real, full speed. And when I slide down, his hand, which is like wet from him being all sweaty, his hand slips and ends up on my boob. On my breast. Not just one hand, but both of them. He says, oops, sorry. Okay, so accidents happen, right? We try it again. The same thing happens. Oops, sorry. We try again. His hands on my breasts. Oops, sorry. The teacher, she's is on the other side of the room. I say to this guy, maybe we don't have this right. Is there something I'm doing? He says, we just have to practice.

And I say, we're practicing it wrong. He shrugs, like, whatever. I get back into position and in the mirror I can see him making a face at another guy, like look at me, dude, like a virtual high five. Just my luck to partner with the only straight male dancer at the conference. He says, are we gonna try it again? What I want to do is when I'm sliding down is hook my foot into the waistband of his pants and ull his pants down with my toe, pull down his pants in front of everybody. Oops, sorry. But I don't do that. I don't do anything.

Dramatic
Miranda, mid to late teens

Miranda shares with the audience her puzzlement with guys' attitude towards sex.

MIRANDA: What I really want to say is that guys hate girls. They wouldn't do stuff if they didn't hate us, right? Why does someone… I don't get it. He has to hate me to do something like that. But if he wants me, then he likes me? It's just so messed up. What kind of fun is it for a guy, knowing a girl is only letting, well, not letting, but that the only reason he's having sex with her is because she's like so out of it, so drugged that she doesn't know what's going on. How can that be fun? Tell me. How can that be a good time? And how can he think other guys are going to think he's… and they do. They like high five each other. Like, man, he got some. Got some what? What did he get? What's in it for him? You think he likes you, but if he likes me he would never… I don't get it. Will I ever get it? So he tries something, thinks he got somewhere... What do I do when I see him coming down the hall? I used to like that smile, the one that all of a sudden, when he'd see me, he'd be thinking about something and all of a sudden he'd see me, he'd notice me and there'd be this smile, happy to see me. Was he smiling that night? When he tried to.... when he.... What happened that night?

Comic
Babette, twenties

Babette is meeting her husband, Harry, for lunch. She
has discovered his secret and is pissed.

BABETTE: Harry. You cannot build a marriage on lies and
deceit. Hookers I can deal with. But this ... this ... I found
your birth certificate, Harry. I lost my car keys and I was
looking around in your drawer to see if maybe you had an
extra set and I found it, your goddamn birth certificate.
You lied to me, Harry. You're not seventy-two like you
said you were. You're only fifty-six. I cried, Harry. For
thirty minutes straight, I cried. Do you realize what this
means Harry? Do you? You're probably going to live sixteen more years then I counted on. I've Googled it, Harry.
The average man dies at seventy-eight. And you take such
goddamn good care of yourself you'll probably make it
to eighty-four. Eighty-four, Harry. That›s twenty-eight
years away. Oh, my God, Harry, when you check out I›ll
almost be in my fifties. Where is my future then? It›s over
for us, Harry. I married you because I thought you were
old. My dreams of being a rich, young widow have been
shattered, Harry. Shattered by a man I trusted, a man I
believed in. Oh, Harry, you›re not going to die for a long,
long time and when you finally do, I'm going to be an
old, old widow.

For information on this author, click on the
WRITERS tab at www.smithandkraus.com.

Comic
Debbie, late twenties

> *Debbie, an actress who appears to be in her late 20s,*
> *is meeting with her agent, who has pleaded with her*
> *to stop having plastic surgery. She refuses. Turns out,*
> *she's a lot older than she looks.*

DEBBIE: No. No Michael, I'm sorry but I'm not going to listen to you. I'm going to continue having plastic surgery and I'm going to continue looking as young as I can. That's the business I'm in Michael and no matter how old I get nobody's pushing me out. Not you, not Doctor Persky, not Meryl Streep, not Hannah Montana, that little shit, nobody. If you want to accept this getting old crap go right ahead, but I'm going to fight for my youth every minute I can, because you know what I think aging is? Aging is what happens when you allow it to happen. Well, that's one thing I'm not doing. I'm hanging in there kicking and screaming and remaining as young and vibrant as I can because that's what I'm all about and that's what I'm going to be all about till the day I'm six feet under. Sorry I can't stay for the lemon. I have a Pilates class in fifteen minutes. So long Michael. You can grow old if you want to, but don't count on me buying into it.

For information on this author, click on the
WRITERS tab at www.smithandkraus.com.

LADY MACBETH AND HER LOVER

Richard Vetere

Dramatic
Hope, early thirties

> *Hope is speaking to her significant other and fellow poetess Corrine who she has broken off. The scene occurs only moments before Hope accidentally overdoses on pills and alcohol. Hope is in an unhappy marriage and struggles fiercely with being a mother of a young girl since it interferes with her writing her poetry. Corrine has just told Hope that she is obsessed with her mother. Hope denies that she is but clearly goes on to reveal that she is obsessed with her mother.*

HOPE: Don't tell me about how I feel about my mother. She stole from us. And what she didn't steal, she shot up her arm. I hated her. That's what she did to the people in her life. She made them become obsessed with her. I outlived her, you know. She was what thirty-one when they found her under the Brooklyn Bridge. Thirty-one she was. Shot dead in a drug deal. Bitch. *(Pause)* I'm thirty-one and two months. *(Pause)* A lovely bitch she was. I counted the days she was around. I used to sit by her door waiting for her to get up. Sometimes she didn't wake up until four. In the winter, it was already dark. But I waited just to watch her wash her face in the sink. Just to watch her go to the bathroom and look at me from across the room with those bleary eyes. And in them I saw all the darkness from the night before. Everything she lived, I saw in those eyes. Humiliation. Shame. Regret.

(then with awe)

My God, I adored her. She moved through my little life like a mountain. Her quiet was like a fire. Burned my father so bad he ran away and never came back. She bit my lip once to watch me bleed. God, no wonder men killed over her. No wonder they killed her.

(Beat)

She loved me, didn't she?

Dramatic
Corinne, thirty

> *Corinne is speaking to her significant other and fellow*
> *poetess Hope as she tries to convince her to commit*
> *suicide with her. Hope has abandoned Corrinne, is*
> *a mother of a young daughter and in an unhappy*
> *marriage. Corinne is explaining to Hope that Hope's*
> *mother did not love Hope and the god Hope is obsessed*
> *with is just like her mother — indifferent to Hope's exis-*
> *tence. Corinne then tries to talk Hope into committing*
> *suicide with her because they love one another her and*
> *it is best to die when still beautiful and desirable.*

CORINNE: At the best, you were an amusement to her. The
worse, you were a drag on her existence. She left you
with the foster parents, no? She loved you? How the fuck
can you ask that? Every time you get high you gotta talk
about how God is looking down on you and ask if your
mother loved you? No to both questions. Your iniquitous,
cretinous God doesn't exist and your mother couldn't pretend to love you even if they paid her. I told you before.
Nobody can hate their mothers. It's against our genetic
code. Sure people whine about it and they write about
mother hatred but in the end it's impossible to hate the
womb you popped out of. Despite the bitch the womb
belongs to. She'd take all the credit. She said she made
you suffer and now you got something out of it by turning
that suffering into art. Think of what she'd be like if she
was alive today. Some old lady with white eyes. So mean
and nasty, she'd be in handcuffs in some institution for the
safety of other living beings. *(Pause)* At least that's how
I see her the way you talk about her. *(Pause)* I'll give her
this though, your mother knew it was better to go out like

a falling star. A bright flash in the great darkness. That's how we should go. When we are still young enough to matter. Young enough that people look at us. The disappointment is ahead of us, you know that. It's all ahead

Lady Macbeth And Her Lover
Richard Vetere

Dramatic
Corinne, forty-five to fifty

> *Corinne is opening her heart to Emily who is her significant other, Hope's daughter. Emily has come to Corinne's home out of the blue to ask her to mentor her so she can be as great a poet as her mother Hope was. Emily looks exactly like her mother Hope who Corinnee adored. Corrine wants Emily to be her lover and in return she will help Emily become a great poet.*

CORINNE: Though I don't believe in God, I have sins. Since I don't believe in an afterlife, I suffer in this one more than those who do believe. Because this is all I have. I never thought I'd see your mother again, and here she is. Younger than I am. What a curse that is on me, don't you understand? It's you I have feelings for. *(Pause)* Become the poet she was. Love the woman she did. *(Pause)* You came here with a purpose. Once you get here you look around this room and you see not only your mother everywhere, but also, yourself. It's as if I built an altar to you as well as her. Do you know why I have all these photos of her? *(Pause)* There is an Arabic saying that when God sent Lucifer to hell Lucifer froze the words "Go to Hell." Lucifer loved God so much that he couldn't bear being in a world without the presence of God. So in the cold depths of hell the only place in existence without God's presence Lucifer kept close the presence of God by freezing his condemnation. You want to be a great poet, do what your mother did. Love me. I am your muse. *(Pause)* Cherish your muse. Give them your heart and soul. *(Pause)* A poet suffers because they need to find impossible ways of sharing their suffering and turning it into beauty. *(Pause)* Think deeply of how your fellow students feared you. Wanted to be you. Resented you. Admired you. All in the same moment. That is ambition. "And though her body dies, her fame survives..." Milton. *(Pause)* Roam the world a second-rate poet. Live in your mother's shadow. Or emerge from it. Either love me or leave my house.

Dramatic
Chrissy, late thirties

> *Chrissy, an acting teacher, is speaking to Gen, one of*
> *her students, who is known as "Silent Gen" because*
> *she doesn't speak. Gen wasn't always called Silent*
> *Gen. It became her nickname after she witnessed her*
> *friend and collaborator fall from a window to her death*
> *while rehearsing for Chrissy's class. After that, Gen*
> *stopped speaking, taking a vow of silence of sorts. It*
> *is now Gen's senior year and in order to graduate, she*
> *must perform a final scene. Though Chrissy has a deep*
> *understanding of the reason for Gen's silence, she can't*
> *pass her without her performing a final scene, which*
> *will require her to speak.*

CHRISSY: Thanks for coming in, Gennifer. You can take
a seat. As you know, we are coming up on final scene
day, and I know that you haven't picked a partner. I
had to reassign Jacob because he said you...well...
weren't...cooperating. *(Beat)* I respect your deci-
sion...your commitment to stay within the Drama
major after the...incident. Your written work. Is.
Breathtaking. Truly. Outstanding. And I'm not just
saying that. I absolutely think you have a strong and
unique... Voice. *(Beat)* While acting has never been
your focus, you've been told that participating in the final Senior Scene day is a requirement for graduation. I
don't make the rules. It's a requirement. I already said
that. What I mean to say is... I need you to- You've
got to- *(Beat)* You're going to have to speak. I know
that you have been through a lot during your time
here. What I mean to say is, I am willing to talk. I am
willing to talk about other options.

(CHRISSY looks at GEN for a long beat, until she realizes:)

What I mean to say is, you've been through something that is very…unique. That is maybe not the right… The correct…. Word. I understand. I was there myself during the … accident. I saw it happen. And it was my class you were rehearsing for, which I'm sure you remember. And I have…. I do… Understand. Perhaps not like you do. But I understand. Something. *(Beat)* The assignment only requires you to do a scene, off-book. Even memorizing a sonnet. How about a poem? *(Beat)* Look, I'm being more than fair. There are the rules. When you leave this college, you will be expected to speak at any job you apply for. I would be sending you out into the world unprepared. And what happened was … horrible. Heart breaking … Senseless… Um. What happened. There is no word. For what happened. No words. But what happens in the rest of the world is cruel too. And if you want to be sent out there with a college degree? You are going to have to participate in Final Scene day with the rest of your classmates. I don't suppose you have a suggestion on how you might do that without saying a word.

LIVE FROM THE SURFACE OF THE MOON
Max Baker

Comic
June, twenty-seven

> *June and her husband Wendell have been invited to Don and Carol's house on the night of July 20, 1969, to watch the moon landing on TV. There they meet Holly, a potential babysitter for Carol who is nine months pregnant. Carol's father, Joe is also present. They are having drinks before the meatloaf Carol has prepared. June has the floor.*

JUNE: I plan all our meals two weeks in advance - The less time I have to spend shopping the better, it's so much easier that way. So I'm in Fisher Foods picking out tomatoes and this man comes up to me - this Store Manager type man - And he comes up behind him, I hear him, and he says "Ma'am,- He calls me "ma'am" "Ma'am - you can't be picking every piece of fruit with your bare hands". And he has on a bright red shirt and tan pants. Only the thing about this man was: He was a midget. And I don't just mean short - I've seen plenty of short men - this man was a midget. And he had a label on his shirt that said Produce Manager on it. And I'm standing there with a tomato in each hand being scolded by this midget Manager Man. I'm telling you he was so short. Well - I started laughing. And that only made him more hacked and shout even louder I tell you, he was eating grapes off of the wallpaper, and the angrier he got the funnier I thought he was. Only when I got home I felt bad. I felt terrible actually. Because - goodness - what must he feel like? And - well - I'm sure we've all felt like that at some point, so, compassion, compassion, compassion, but - he was just so small you know. So small. And I don't see how anyone that small gets to be

a Produce Manager at Fisher Foods. Fisher Foods! That's
a lot of responsibility.

Dramatic
Maggie, mid-thirties

Maggie tells her ex-husband Lou's new wife Penny why she finally had to call it quits with him. Erica is their daughter.

MAGGIE: He tell you how he used to drink so much he'd shit in our bed? Often enough I kept a box of Hefty bags by the nightstand so I could throw the sheets in there before they smelled the whole fuckin' house up. Or how about that night I come home, and there's Lou, sitting there on the floor, puke all down front of his uniform, so drunk I gotta blink my eyes to see through the fucking whisky stench and he's bear-hugging Erica so tight she's choking. He's so cocked, he can't tell that he has his arm jammed around her throat and she ain't breathing. Erica... she's a little thing, all legs and elbows and Lou's always been so strong, especially when he has some drink in him and... she's turning grey in the face and I say "Lou, let her the go!" and I start pulling his arms but he's so fucking hammered he doesn't see me, won't let her go. I slap him, kick him, I'm this close to pulling the piece off his hip and shooting his fucking kneecap but instead I pull a big chunk of hair and skin off of his head an' only then –bleeding from his scalp— does he let her go. And what does he do? Does he apologize? Does he ask how Erica is? As she's gasping for her life, he curls in the fetal position and pisses himself. Up to me to get her calm. Up to me to clean the piss and the puke and the blood. Up to me to call his cop buddies so they can cart him off, clean him up, act like nothing ever fucking happened. 'Cause that's what cops do for each other. Us? We're just his family. My mother always says "Boys will be boys. They always come back." We don't see him for three days. Then he comes back, drunk again, slamming on the door. "Lemme in, Mags!" I switched the locks, of course. Erica's shaking, she's fucking scared of him. I don't blame her, bruises on her neck still purple. So I stick a butcher knife through the screen door and I say, real calm, "You take one more step and I'll kill ya." And I meant it with every inch of me. Did he tell you that, Penny? Huh?

Dramatic
Helen, fifty-one.

*Helen's partner of twenty years was Susan, and together
they have a daughter, Clementine. Months have passed
since Susan died unexpectedly in minor surgery. Clementine confronts Helen, arguing that to move through
her grief Helen must begin by opening the hospital
bag of Susan's belongings. Clementine has demanded
to know what her mother thinks or fears might be in
the bag.*

HELEN: I know what's in there! On top, her sandals. The
ones with the hand-painted birds on the—she'd have
taken them off last, they'll be on top—on top of her
blue and white-striped seersucker dress. It'll be shoved
in there. She'd never have folded it. You think I don't
know exactly what she looked like? And, and in her
pockets—I know: her phone; her watch; her wallet,
with something like four dollars inside. She always had
some useless amount—so four dollars, two credit cards,
a bankcard, her library card, and her license—don't you
think I know what's in the bag? Her hair was up when
we went to the hospital. I'm sure they made her take it
down. So that wooden clip—the one from Madrid—will
be in her pocket. With her, her ring… Then she'll have
something random—I mean, always—she had something
completely random in her pocket. THAT will be the only
mystery in the bag. What random something—that she
picked up who knows where—there'll be like a, like a
paper clip. Or a button. Something—one mystery, that's
it, because everything else I know. It's the last time I saw
her. I KNOW she isn't coming back; you think I don't
know? I, I see her walking off with that nurse—over and

over again I see her walking off! She looked back at me–
–I, I don't know what I said to her. What did I?—I don't
know if I said 'I love you.' Or, or, something practical.
Something horribly *useless*, right as she left me. I can't
remember, do you know? Help me? Do you remember?
I said something—help me? What did I say to her?

For information on this author, click on the
WRITERS tab at www.smithandkraus.com.

Comic
Kira, early twenties

> *Kira Haskell, in her early twenties, tries to convince Terry Winters, an unsuccessful garage door salesman in his mid-twenties, not to leave town until he gives their friendship a chance to possibly lead to romance.*

KIRA: Since you've decided to leave town so abruptly, I think we need to cut to the chase. Look, I'm not saying a romance is definitely going to happen between us and maybe, like you said, this could be just a rebound from a failed relationship, although I don't think it is. But I'm sure we both agree that we have become friends and sometimes friends do become more than friends and I think if that's possible it's something we'd be foolish not to pursue, unless one of us isn't that interested in carrying this friend thing any further than just being friends, which, although it's definitely not the way I feel, I would totally understand if it's the way you feel and although, yes, I would be greatly disappointed, at least I would be relieved knowing that I did everything possible I could to convince you to stay and give it a chance to see where it's going, which I feel is so worth it that I'm even willing to resort to coming off as a desperate, pathetic, brainless, babbling idiot as I am now doing because if I don't and you leave town without knowing all this, then I would feel even worse than I feel right now having to say all this. So there! How's that!

For information on this author, click on the WRITERS tab at www.smithandkraus.com.

Dramatic
Mia, thirty-eight

> *Mia is an actress who is on a home shopping TV show.*
> *Her boyfriend, Johnny, wants her to have a baby. They've*
> *tried – but so far, no-go. Here, she explains to him why she*
> *has decided that she doesn't want to have a kid.*

MIA: All day I worry. All night I worry. About everything. Cancer. Terrorism. Bedbugs. Economic recessions. Getting fired. Falling behind. Food with unspecified calorie counts. The hygiene of the person who used the leg press before me. Getting a chip before my next manicure that I'll have to stare at and obsess over until the moment it's repaired. Random acts of gang-related violence. An air conditioner falling on my head...You falling out of love with me. And raising a kid. Raising a kid that ends up hating me. Raising a kid that ends up crazy. Not getting to raise a kid because it's stillborn. Or me dying during child birth and not being there to raise it so it spends its whole life without a mother's love and so will never be happy because of an emotional deficit that can never be filled. That's not even the whole list. *(Pause)* Half the time I think people only want kids as a do-over for their shitty life. I'd just want the thing to go to Juilliard to make me feel better that I didn't...I didn't even know what Juilliard was until I was 30. I don't want to end up divorced and alone with a kid, dad's nowhere to be found, and wind up getting remarried to the first alcoholic with a beard I can find just to fill the space in the living room like my mother did.

> For information on this author, click on the
> WRITERS tab at www.smithandkraus.com.

Dramatic
Lizzy, thirties to forties, southern

Lizzy sits on a porch swing late one evening and opens up to her neighbor Jack (who she believes is asleep) about a romantic encounter she had at her brother's wedding in Savannah.

LIZZY: I went by the school today. Looks like I'll be starting back after the summer. Oooh, they had so many questions. Don't worry. I protected your reputation. Bob Searcy asked me out for coffee. I declined. I guess that's the one good thing about being a grieving widow, you can just... blame it on death. He said I have nice legs... for a Baptist. I baked him a casserole. It seemed like the appropriate response. I don't remember the last time I was on any kind of date. Okay, I won't lie. I do remember. Six years ago, July 3rd, over on Tybee Island in Savannah. My brother's wedding. There was a groomsman. Michael. We danced at the wedding, snuck out, went over to the beach and watched the sun go down. Talked and talked. He told me he had big plans to open his own hardware business, and I told him he could do it too and he believed me. And then there was the not talking. It was like falling... falling and falling, over and over - like we'd always have that moment - and I could just die right then and there, because nothing else mattered. In the morning we walked over to the coffee shop and got breakfast. And we walked out onto the pier for a while... fed the seagulls. He pulled me into him and I put my head on his chest and he said... *I won't forget you. (A whisper)* I won't forget you.... *(Beat)* And then he kissed me and left for California. I knew we'd keep in touch, I just knew we would... but he... he told me his life was complicated, some girl back home. And he never made any promises to me, so, I told myself I had no right to feel anything. I still do that, by the way. It's a neat little game I play with myself. But you know, I wonder sometimes, if there was a way of wiping that memory away, would I do it? I don't know what's worse... to have a moment like that and lose it... or to go through life in the dark. One thing I do know. I don't trust any of it. Not anymore. Because walks on the beach at twilight... they don't mean anything. It seems as if they must, but they don't.

Dramatic

Lizzy, thirties to forties southern

Lizzy, slightly inebriated, talks with her neighbor Jack about her unhappy marriage and the death of her husband Jesse.

LIZZY: I was faithful. I was a good wife. He gave me something solid, something real. I didn't want a divorce. I don't believe in it. And so I sat him down one night and I told him if he needed that... if he needed to go and find that somewhere else, I wouldn't stop him. And it was awful. He was so angry. He started yelling at me, said it was a crime against God what I was doing. I said, but I can't give you what I don't have, I can't feel what I don't feel. I said, what do you want me to do, just lay there and lie to you? He threw his plate across the kitchen. We didn't talk for weeks. When summer came around, I noticed he was working longer hours, coming home late. And then one night I heard him leave the bed around midnight. And I knew he was - I smelled his cologne. But I didn't say a word. In my head I was like... yes. Go. Go do... what you need to do. He came back a few hours later like nothing had happened... he put his hand on my shoulder, like he always does, but I laid real still... waited for him to fall asleep. And then I went downstairs and sat at the kitchen table for a while... watched the sun come up. Cooked him some eggs and he came down and we sat there and ate. Total silence. And then when he stood up to go to work he kissed me on my forehead and said I love you. And I looked up at him... all the color just drained right out of his face... the sadness of a million days and him knowing I'd resent him for it, but it wadn't that at all. I just didn't want it floatin' around in my head. That's what I wanted to tell him, but I didn't say a word. He went off to work down to that roofing job in Opelika and I sat there at the table... fell asleep, I guess, I don't know how long I slept, but I woke up to a phone call from Mr. Ledbetter: Jesse took a fall. I didn't even cry at the funeral. What kinda of woman... I know how to love, I do. I just didn't know how to love him. He was a good man. He was such a good man. And now, I feel like I'm surrounded by all these people, all over town –

(mimicking)

Oh, Lizzy, I'm so sorry…

(beat)

But they don't know! I've destroyed lives, Mr. Key. Whole lives!

Seriocomic

Lizzy, thirties to forties, southern

> *Lizzy is shaken from just being kissed by her neighbor Jack.*

LIZZY: I told my pastor I was having impure thoughts about a Maytag dryer. He said there was no such thing. I said but it has a heated steam cycle, and he said, ooooh, there might be something to that. You smell like Joe Namath. I always think of him from those Brut commercials. And when I smell a man that smells good, I always think he might smell like Joe Namath. And then I imagine him in that other commercial with the pantyhose and I get all confused. Mr. Key. You have a Maytag dryer on your porch. It's been out there a year. And I have to ask myself why it doesn't bother me anymore, it hasn't bothered me for a while, actually. You asked me about being happy. But the truth is… I don't remember anything about being happy. I don't know if I've ever been happy. And I'm standing here, and I'm wanting to trust you. I'm wanting to tell you that you're a really good kisser. And that I have feelings for you. Important ones. And that as terrified as I am right now, I really do want more of those kisses. And I'm saying all of this out loud while being fully and completely aware that you may run away. *(Beat)* I'm not imagining this Mr. Key. This is very real, the fears that I have very, very real. Every single time I have reached out for something like this it has fallen right through fingers. And I have to think maybe some people just aren't meant to have the things they want, or to be loved in the way that they ought to. Ya know? I don't want to believe that that's true, but damnit, I see no evidence to the contrary. I'm alone, Mr. Key, and I always have been, and I'm so tired. I'm so tired of waiting... and why- why do men just stand there and let a woman ramble on and on like this?

Comic
Typical Tina, early thirties

> *Typical Tina begrudgingly accepts the nickname her*
> *husband has bestowed upon her despite the fact that*
> *she is anything but 'typical.' She is, in fact, skeptical,*
> *wise, and often sardonic and, when provoked, she is*
> *likely to show her true colors. On this particular oc-*
> *casion, Tina is indeed provoked. After enduring nearly*
> *eight flavorless years of marriage to Normal Ted (a*
> *man in his mid-30s with a middle-managerial desk*
> *job and a lack of lust for life), Tina learns that Guru*
> *Gallagher (a charismatic middle-aged mentalist) has*
> *bilked her husband out of their life savings to pay for*
> *an anti-negativity statue that he claimed would release*
> *Normal Ted of his normalness and turn his life into*
> *something more remarkable. But the veil of magic has*
> *been lifted. Guru Gallagher has been exposed. Normal*
> *Ted has been duped. And Typical Tina is not taking it*
> *anymore. She boldly steps out of her shell to give them*
> *both a piece of her mind and a cosmic reality check*
> *they won't soon forget.*

TYPICAL TINA: Let me get this straight. You told my
husband you detected random waves of negative energy
that were clogging his root chakras and blocking his
soul? And you believed him? Okay, here's what's going to happen. Guru Gallagher, you are taking back this
worthless trinket, and you're giving us our money back.
With interest. That's right, with interest! That seventeen
hundred dollars was our life savings. Do you know what
we could have done with that money? Ted, you *know* I
had my heart set on that hotel suite in the Poconos with

the seven-foot champagne glass whirlpool. We are not going anywhere until you pay us back for your shameless swindle! And that's a small price to pay to keep me from following you from town to town, from psychic fair to psychic fair, tracking your every move, exposing you for the con artist you really are. I will be tireless in my pursuit of debunking, demystifying, and discrediting every last morsel of your paranormal claims, the likes of which turn otherwise normal men into sniveling wannabes… believers of magic and hokum… like Normal Ted here. Always looking for something better around the corner, aren't you, Ted? Always looking for that greener grass, for the supernatural or the otherworldly when –guess what– *this* world right here in front of you is the best one you've got, and it happens to be magnificent. Wake up, Normal Ted. That magic potion you're looking for? It isn't out there. And I refuse to let you waste one more minute of your life – of *our* life – searching for it. From now on, you will choose to celebrate your very existence no matter how normal it feels. You will stop looking for mystical solutions from mind readers and spoon benders and psychic performers to make your life meaningful. Don't you get it? You're already living a charmed life. Because *you* get to live out your days as a little cosmic dust-speck riding bareback on a spinning planet called Earth that silently moves a thousand miles an hour on its axis, at sixty-seven thousand miles per hour around the sun, in a massive interplanetary system that stretches, oh, about seven hundred *billion* miles across oceans of countless stars, in one galaxy among a hundred billion others. *That,* my friend, is as magical as it gets. And I'd say that makes your normal little life pretty flippin' phenomenal.

For information on this author, click on the WRITERS tab at www.smithandkraus.com.

Seriocomic
Zooey

After meeting the man of her dreams during a plane flight, Zooey tells him what she expects from their relationship.

ZOOEY: When I met you and you asked for non-salted peanuts, I couldn't believe it because just hours before I had written a long letter to the management of Delta Airlines suggesting we offer a non-salted option. And then your voice was so soothing, I felt I'd heard it all my life. And then when you said you were an actor, and that you recorded my favorite romance novel *The Thorn Birds,* which I just finished listening to again on my way to the airport, well, I sorta melted. At that moment, I knew that I'd break Delta Airlines rules about having sex with passengers in the bathroom. And now you ask what I want from this chance meeting. I want our story to be just like a romance novel. I want to know that you'll call tomorrow. That we'll date for an appropriate amount of time, maybe three to five chapters. And then at the end of chapter six, you'll take me out to dinner and surprise me with a ring and I'll quit being a flight attendant. And then in chapters seven through fourteen we'll rise above the normal humdrum of existence. We'll also survive that tragic night in chapter nine when your mother dies in that awful train wreck. In chapter ten, our love will rise above my momentary fling with a handsome priest who has been sent into exile at a remote parish for insulting a bishop. Despite the fact that he's sworn to a life of celibacy, he breaks his vows, consummates our passion, and dies of a broken heart. But you forgive my wandering spirit and together we raise the love-child as our own. Years later, in chapter eighteen, on my deathbed, with our children and love-children gathered around us, the music will crest and I'll know that I've lived not a life but a page-turner. That's not too much to ask for is it?

Dramatic
Sharon, thirty-five

> *Sharon has come to Nashville to confront Justin, who*
> *dumped her when he became a country music star and*
> *who is getting married. She doesn't want to stop the*
> *marriage – she just wants an apology and a thank-you*
> *for everything she did for him before he became famous.*
> *She barges into Justin's hotel room but finds, instead, is*
> *Uncle Jim. He doesn't know who she is, but she knows*
> *all about him. Here, she tells whom who she is.*

SHARON: Name is Sharon Mary Warfel, middle child of
Dennis and Inez Warfel. Thirty-five years of age, as of exactly two days ago. I own most of a two-bedroom, ranch-
style home here in Nashville and have been employed by
same city for over five years as a decorated officer of the
law. Like you, also did a stint in the military, also Army.
Three years active duty, but unlike you, I came out with
stripes on my shoulders. Was also engaged to be married, however briefly, to one Justin Eugene Spears, son
of Henry Carl Spears, your brother, making my former
fiancee, lying piece of shit that he is. He's downstairs with
his sycophants, drinking a Corona Light, eating a chimi-
changa and laughing at his own fucking jokes. Recited
your entire life history upon entry, you don't think I know
who's in this fucking building. And if I wanted to kill that
son of a bitch, he'd already be dead. As would the ex-
con-junkie-snitch that I framed into doin' the deed. What
can I tell you, Jim. May I call you Jim? We "scorned
women" handle rejection in a lot of different ways.
Some gals take to the couch, balled-up, crying, watching
"Fried Green Tomatoes" and gnawing on a log of cookie
dough. Others of us buy eleven hundred dollars' worth of

surveillance equipment, study our exes' every waking move, then find a stone-cold-killer-smack-addict who'll cut their "former's" throat from ear to ear, make it look like a failed robbery attempt and won't be missed when they vanish from the face of the fucking earth.

For information on this author, click on the WRITERS tab at www.smithandkraus.com.

Dramatic
Jo, thirty-seven

> Nice Girl *takes place in a small Boston suburb in the 1980's. Jo is talking to Donny, a friend from high school. Neither is happy about the way their life turned out. Jo left college to help her mother after her father died and never went back. Donny got his girlfriend pregnant, married her, and became a butcher like his father.*

JO: I did everything wrong and I'm not happy either so. *(Beat.)* You know what I think? Donny Moretti? I think. I think nobody's happy. I think that's the big joke. From God. Being happy doesn't really exist. Or it does but it's like a scratch off lottery ticket. And most people don't hit the jackpot. I think you get stuff you think you want and you want something else. I think you never get what you think you want and that sucks too. I think life's about always wanting. *Something. (Beat.)* I don't know that I've ever wanted anything. Or if I did? It was so long ago. I don't even remember what it felt like. And so. Maybe I'm not even alive. Maybe I'm dead and just. Walking around. And I don't even know it. *(Beat.)* You ever feel like that? You ever feel like you're walking around dead? Sometimes. Sometimes I pinch myself over and over and over again. Just so I can feel something to remind myself I'm not dead yet. Or I bite my tongue on purpose. Or I stick my finger with a pin just to see it bleed. Something. Anything. Because otherwise I got no solid proof that I. Actually exist. *(Beat.)* Whadya think of that. Huh? Tell me I'm not fucked in the head after hearing *that*.

Dramatic
Helen forty to fifty

*Six years ago, Helen's 10-year-old son Adam acciden-
tally shot and killed her 9-year-old son Joey after she
left a loaded handgun in the kitchen cabinet. Helen is
talking to a social worker who has come to interview
her family to see if Adam, now 16, can be released
from parole.*

HELEN: I know what you're thinking. I can see it in your
eyes. I could see it the moment you walked in. And it's
not what you think. *I'm* not what you think. You just come
in here and judge, judge, judge. And you've got that face
on and those clothes on and you look at me and you look
at my house and I know what you think. But what you
think isn't true. I lost my son. I lost my son. Can you
understand that? Can you hear what I'm saying??? I
LOST MY SON. I killed him. I did. It should have been
me in that jail and not him but nobody would listen
and then they take him. That little boy - he was ten - he
was a ten year old little boy and they tried to make an
example of him. Make an example out of all of us. But
what nobody understands is that I lost my son! You
people are always asking me these questions about what
I've got in my house and I'm telling you that I've only
got the things that I need. Nothing more. My husband is
in the army. He serves his country so don't tell me what
I can't have. Don't try to tell me that! It's like having a
kitchen knife to cut up your - whatever the hell it is that
you people eat your - your salads ... what happened here
was an accident! And we are all just trying to recover
but you come in here with all your judgments and all
you've got to say about whatever it is that you've got to

say but I don't give a shit anymore. All you do is talk. All I hear is you talking but you're not listening to me and you're not listening to my family. We lost somebody. We lost somebody!

For information on this author, click on the WRITERS tab at www.smithandkraus.com.

Dramatic
Kim, thirties

>*Kim (or rather, "The Other Thing" which has taken her over) has come to see Carl. He's a former ghost hunter who's now in an institution because he's had what his doctors think was a stroke and cannot speak or walk; but it wasn't a stroke - "The Other Thing" inside Kim asphyxiated him. She has now come to finish the job.*

KIM: Do you know what little girls are told as they are growing up? Be good. Be nice. Little girls are told to speak their mind, but not too often. They are told to have goals and dreams and desires, but not too many. They are told to say sorry and to make people feel comfortable and to be pretty ancl friendly. To be good. To be nice. And good ancl nice means weaker and smallèr and less than. *(beat)* But. Carl. When you stop being good and nice, you discover that you don't like when people make you feel weak and small and less than. And you aren't going to let anyone make you feel that way again. Not ever again. Because if anyone tries to do that? You obliterate them. *(A long beat)* Oh, don't take it personally, Carl. This isn't a vendetta against you. You may have been the straw that broke the camel's back. You and your ghost hunting business. How important it made you feel explaining all of that to her. To me. Explaining the way the world works, is that right? And who she is in the world and who you are in the world, and what is so and what is not so. Oh, men love explaining things to us. That really pisses me off. *(beat)* But no. You weren't even my first. And you certainly won't be my last. I have been very busy since I left you all those months ago. Years, has it been? I don't know. It cloesn't matter. Because I've been very busy.

And I'm very good at what I do.*(beat)* You know there are more like me. There are many. And we are coming to find all of you. And you aren't hard to find. Don't worry. No one is going to interrupt us. I told them I was your daughter. They didn't even check my ID! Security these days. I thought you'd think that was funny. No? Oh well. *(beat)* Even so. Do you know what happens if I'm caught? It's rare, but do you know?*(beat)* I tell you, it's very interesting, how little anyone suspects the young woman who was merely in the wrong place at the wrong time. After all, how could a girl like me dream of attacking anyone, especially such strong men? Not that you're a strong man, Carl. You, they won't even question. All of a sudden, a stricken young woman running into the lobby, screaming "someone help! Help! He's not breathing!" *(beat)*It is amazing. What can be borne from outrage. *(beat)* We are coming — all of us — to take away this hold that you have over the world. And it will be unpleasant. For men like you. (beat) Men like you don't really matter. That's the big secret. Despite how you move through this world as if you are all that matters. And despite how the world moves for you, at your every whim. The things you can get away with in this world! I swear. And you don't evàn know that you're cloing it. None of you even know that you're doing it. *(beat)* If you think a war is coming, You are very wrong. The war is here. And men like you are going to lose. *(beat)* No, Carl. You really don't matter. Not a single bit.

Comic
Penelope, sixteen

> *Penelope and her best friend Lucius have gone to*
> *Ithaca Falls on a hot summer night and run into*
> *their classmate Odysseus, who is skinny dipping*
> *and smoking weed. Penelope is instantly attracted*
> *to Odysseus, much to Lucius' dismay. In this mono-*
> *logue Penelope needs Lucius to leave so she can be*
> *alone with Odysseus and hopefully be kissed for the*
> *first time in her life.*

PENELOPE: I'm sorry Lucius. You're right, I'm just - I'm
kind of stoned now and Odysseus - ok, Odysseus is
- I've never told you this but I have such a crush on
Odysseus Johnson I cannot handle it. I think he's so
hot. Do you think he's into me? I can't tell. He's very
aloof. But so interesting. I've always thought he was
interesting. Have you ever seen him running? He's a
beautiful runner. He has such a beautiful body. Like
a God. He runs everywhere, I think he's like a long
distance runner or something. He's always running
with his shirt off, except in the winter duh, then he has
a shirt on, but he totally runs by my house all the time.
I love watching him run. Even Aunt Peggy who's as
dykey as they come, has to catch her breath when he
runs by the house. I'm going to try to kiss him tonight.
Or get him to kiss me I mean. No one has ever kissed
me Lucius and tonight is the night! I can feel it! I think
you should totally either come in the water right now
or you should go so I can be alone with Odysseus. I
mean, I don't want to be rude or anything but you're
kind of being a buzzkill and that's - I'm being rude.
We're still best friends, this is just- like - I don't know

- I'm having a total experience right now.

For information on this author, click on the WRITERS tab at www.smithandkraus.com.

PENELOPE OF ITHACA
Kenny Finkle

Dramatic
Peggy Fontaine, fifty to sixty-five (her age is a mystery in the play)

> *Peggy is an outspoken, tough, dynamic community leader and weaver. She has raised her niece Penelope as her own after Penelope's parents died. When Penelope's husband Odysseus tells Peggy that he is going to join the army, Peggy is furious. She needs to convince Odysseus to stay in Ithaca and fight for freedom in his own backyard.*

PEGGY: Penelope knows this but you don't and it's high time you did... I am the Original Wild Woman of Ithaca. Oh yes. Everyone will tell you. Go on and ask people. They'll tell you - I've fought to preserve the quality of this fine city all my adult life. I've fought the big fights, I've walked the walk, I haven't always won but winning isn't the point, it's the fight that matters. The fight! I've fought the infiltration of big business, I demanded new school curricula, I've fought for solar energy and to keep the trees up near Cornell and not to turn the whole damn city into a parking lot, I've lead rallies, organized demonstrations, staged sit ins, made giant peace signs that planes could see flying by. I'm the reason that Ithaca is the way it is...except for the bad things, I'm not responsible for those. But even those I suppose I allowed so I must take responsibility for them too. What I'm trying to get at is I know what it means to need to fight enemies Odysseus, to feel that there's injustice and wrong in the world but if you want to fight, stay here and fight for things that will impact your wife and your child and your child's children. Fight here. We could fight together Odysseus.

For information on this author, click on the
WRITERS tab at www.smithandkraus.com.

Dramatic
Penelope, thirty-six

> *Penelope and her best friend Lucius have been es-*
> *tranged for almost 20 years. In those years Penelope*
> *has waited for her husband Odysseus to return from*
> *a war. She has raised their son Telemachus with the*
> *help of her Aunt Peggy. After Peggy's funeral, Lucius*
> *re-appears in Penelope's life and the two find them-*
> *selves on the precipice of love. Penelope needs Lucius*
> *to kiss her.*

PENELOPE: You – you've been – I'm so happy you're here.
And - you're so good with him. With Telemachus. And
me. You're so good with me. You've changed Lucius.
You're stronger now. You've gotten stronger and I've
gotten weaker. I used to think I was stronger but I'm not.
Sometimes I wonder what would happen if we kissed.
Sometimes I think we should make love. Sometimes I
think about that. About what would happen if we made
love. Sometimes I think about making love to you. I think
about what your body would feel like with mine. How
you would kiss me. How you would hold me. How you
would feel inside me. I think about what you look like
with your clothes off. I look at your body through your
clothes all the time. Do you look at mine? You do. I see
you do it. Over dinner or when we're sitting on the couch
or that day we went hiking at Buttermilk Falls. Do you
remember that day? It was so hot and we jumped in the
water really quickly and then kept hiking. I know you
were looking at me that day. I could see that you were
excited. I saw you try to hide it. I let you hide it. I didn't
want you to hide it. I wanted you to take me the way
you took me that night at the Waterfalls years ago. That

scared me then but now it's all I wish for. For you to take me like that. Would you take me like that again? You'd have to take me like that because otherwise it won't ever happen. I can't let it happen. I can't be the one to make it happen. It has to be you because I'm supposed to be the one that's waiting for her husband to come back. That's who I am. That's what people have made me. That's what I made myself and I didn't mean to. I didn't know that I'd have to wait this long or that the waiting would turn into something else and that I'd become this person, this woman with all this passion and desire and love and soul and no way to get it out. I would have done everything differently if I knew this would be how I feel because Lucius I can't live like this any longer. I can't live with all this inside me. I can't live waiting for him to come home anymore. I need release. I need to be free. I need to breathe. Will you give me some of your breath? Will you breathe into my mouth and give me back some life? Just a kiss. That's all I need. A kiss would sustain me. I know it would. That's all I need. A kiss. Will you kiss me Lucius. Please. As my friend. As a man. Please.

For information on this author, click on the WRITERS tab at www.smithandkraus.com.

Dramatic

> *Beverly, 30-50, ageless, pragmatic. She works as a general office administrator and is speaking to the audience from her desk.*

BEVERLY: This is a job. I don't believe in the idea of a career. Something that defines you and that you put your heart and soul into because it says something about who you are. Something the success of which you might get confused with your own. I'm successful if I get up every day and put my face on and get to work on time and do my job without ripping a hem or losing an earring. That's it. If I keep my earrings, I am on top. I pity those who aren't like me. Who deeply care about what happens in this office. I say, did you forget to bring a tampon? No? Then it was a good day. Did you drink coffee without burning your mouth or spilling on your sweater? Excellent. Did the café on the corner have your favorite snack? Little things. What can I say? I'm easy. We all have a sob story. Some horrible thing that happened that fucked us up forever. But I'm not telling mine. It's personal. It's probably like everyone else's, really, when you boil it down. I don't flatter myself that I am the only one who suffers. Do you? Do you say, oh poor me, sure other people have problems, but they don't feel them as deeply as I do. I had a roommate like that. She owned three copies of *The Bell Jar.* It was not a great time in either of our lives. We appeared fine, fantastic even, well-educated, cheap rent, living the dream in the big city. NOT. We had so much potential, we were so frickin' potentially great, despite our crappy entry level jobs and our loveless weekends. We knew we were the cream of the crop, and the wrongness of that, the incongruity with reality, almost crushed us. Our brains. But she, in addition to the mental malaise we both suffered from, had chronic fatigue syndrome, so no matter what my problems were, hers trumped 'em. She could not get out of bed. Epstein-Barr virus. Ha, I thought. What's that? Everything's always worse for you, isn't it? Many years later, I had a terrible flu and could barely move my limbs, and I lay there and thought, ohh. This must be how Kate felt. And I was sorry I didn't cook her dinner a couple times. But. C'est la vie. I was scared to talk to her, how was I supposed to cook her dinner? All that darkness. Bad enough to deal with mine. But you're not gonna hear a sob story from me. Because honestly, you could trump it. There are worse things in heaven and earth than have been experienced by me. You're not hearing any of this, by the way, because I'm not talking to you. I'm doing intake, checking the email. I'm making it through my day with a moderate level of competence and that is how I do it. You might want more out of your life. But you won't be happy.

Dramatic
Vicky, mid twenties, British.

> *Vicky is street-smart, a survivor. Sheorks with an escort service in Brighton and Hove, a typical English seaside town. She's talking to Bertie, having arrived at the house at night, in the rain.*

VICKY: Escort. Bleedin' escort agency. The look on your face! Honestly I think I'm better off operating on my own, y'know, on the streets. Some drunk tosser in the back of a pub wants a hand job in the toilet - money up front - cut and dried innit. None of this "pretend you're my niece" shit. They're the real sickos. Agency calls it role-playing, I call it sick in the bleedin' head. Something wrong with you. Look at me - I'm still shaking. If he shows up here - right - if he - if he comes here no matter what he says right, don't let him in? Yeah? Promise me. Promise. I shoulda known - after last week-end. But I thought, you know: it's not like he hurt me or nothing. Didn't even wanna a blow-job or nothing— kisses me on the cheeks when he says goodbye. So I'm thinking yeah - he's a bit weird - but - So - he asks for me again, and they keep promoting repeat customers y'know - but underneath there's this other little voice in my head saying: "Don't Do It Vicky - Don't Bloody Do It". We all got those voices - we all got 'em - Telling us what we know, but we don't listen to 'em do we. We don't bloody listen. *(beat)* So this time he says 'I'll pick you up after school' I'm still playing along like I'm his niece or whatnot - Picks me up, takes me to this broken down boarding house off the London Road, don't know where the fuck I am. Leads me into the back room. Peeling wallpaper, broken windows, there's a bucket in the corner to catch the drips.

Mattress on the floor. So - okay - I get it - another day at the office, let's get it over with. I lie down - next thing I know his hands are round my neck. Pressing in. I'm thinking 'Oy! What the bleedin' hell d'you think you;re playing at?' But he keeps going. And it's getting Harder and harder. And all of a sudden there's this look in his eyes like – like I never seen before - like he was peaceful or something. By now it's like, you know, I'm thinking "This knob-head's gonna kill me!" And the other voice is saying: "I told ya Vicky, I told ya not to trust this fuck, now what are you going to do? Die?" And I'm like, No, no I'm not gonna be strangled to death by this piece of shit pervert on a dirty mattress in the back room of some boarding house on the London Road. So instead of trying to get his hands off from around my neck so I can fucking breathe, I grabbed his balls. And then squeezed 'em really fucking hard. Hard as I could. Well, he makes a noise like a slaughtered pig. Never heard nothing like that before. Grabs his cock, and I high-tail out the front door. Don't know where the bloody hell I am, mind. But I hear him coming after me, so I scarper. Up and down lanes, in and out. Trying to lose him. That's when I find myself at the bottom of your street. I think yeah I know this place. This is where I was last week. Blue front door. He won't think of looking for me here, yeah? I'm safe here. Right? He's not going to think of looking for me here why would he?

For information on this author, click on the WRITERS tab at www.smithandkraus.com.

Dramatic
Elizabeth, fifties

> *Elizabeth is a mother in her 50s from Chicago who lost*
> *her only daughter, Tracy, three years ago. She has sur-*
> *prised Tracy's former college roommate, Kelly, with an*
> *unannounced visit to Kelly's California apartment. She*
> *has just confronted Kelly with a pride flag that was sent*
> *to her after her daughter's death. She has asked Kelly*
> *if she and Tracy were lovers in college. After initially*
> *denying it, Kelly confirms that they were lovers and*
> *that Tracy didn't want Elizabeth to know.*

ELIZABETH: I was having a phone conversation with her once. A few months before she died. Just before Valentine's Day. I said something like, "Hey, Kiddo. Why don't we surprise Daddy by flying you out for a weekend? You can be his Valentine." We both knew that I was the one who wanted her. Daddy would peck her on the cheek, grunt, fart a little less because she was home, and stay glued to college basketball on ESPN. . . . But I would come alive again. Getting her room ready. Cooking for her. Getting my hair and nails done. You have to try and look nice with a young daughter to compete with—naturally! ... Christ . . . My looks went down the toilet when she died. . . . She said she couldn't get away. She had to study. And I heard giggling. But not from her. From someone else in the room. A female voice. But so close to the phone. Like someone had their mouth very near hers. And Tracy said, "shush." Softly. Like she was talking to a child or a small animal. Just "shush." Very tender. And I guess I knew. But I didn't say anything. Because I hoped I was wrong. Instead, I told a long story about the neighbor's cat, Mrs. Fuzzface. How one day

Mrs. Fuzzface had been sleeping on the top of our van. And I drove off with her still up there, not realizing. And a truck driver on the freeway started honking at me and pointing. And I pulled over and there was Mrs. Fuzzface staring down at me. Scared me to death. But not her. She was sort of exhilarated, as near as I could tell from the expression on her little feline face. Exhilarated at getting away with such a stunt. And Tracy laughed. But not the precious laugh she usually had for Mrs. Fuzzface. The laugh that reminded me of her first baby laughs. No. A grown-up laugh. Deeper. Longer. Throaty. Delighted with herself. And I knew. So I said goodbye, and I hung up.

Dramatic
Elizabeth, fifties

> *Elizabeth is a mother in her 50s from Chicago who lost her only daughter, Tracy, three years ago. She has surprised Tracy's former college roommate, Kelly, with an unannounced visit to Kelly's California apartment. Tracy died violently in Colombia while participating in a protest that Kelly arranged and seduced her into joining. Kelly has just asked Elizabeth if she blames her for Tracy's death.*

ELIZABETH: Of course I blame you. . . . My daughter was a literature major when she met you. She was reading Fanny Burney and discovering that feminist novels predate Jane Austen. It was a beautiful moment in her life. Her cheeks were always the shade of red you see on china dolls. She looked good in Abercrombie & Fitch, like a model. She was going to a student-led bible study. She voted republican like her father and me. She had a crush on a boy who worked as a sports' editor on the college newspaper. What the hell happened to that boy? Where did he go? Jesus, did he just disappear? Sometimes I spend whole days fantasizing about that boy. I don't remember his name. Philip? Peter? Jonathan? I fantasize that he got her pregnant. That he got her hooked on drugs. That he beat her. That she became so crazy about him she dropped out of school. I come up with every bad situation I can think of that two young kids could get into. And in the fantasy I fly down to California and save her. Abort the unwanted brat, lock her ass in rehab, set him up with anger management classes, or hire someone from Soldier of Fortune magazine to break his kneecaps. I want that boy for her. Because I can think of a thousand ways the little punk might have ruined her life. But he wouldn't have ended it! He wouldn't have taken her where you took her. Not that boy. Not whatshisname.

Dramatic
Kelly, mid-twenties

> *Kelly, 20s, is a grant writer and former activist living*
> *in Los Angeles. Elizabeth, the mother of Kelly's former*
> *lover Tracy, has surprised Kelly by flying out from*
> *Chicago for an unannounced visit. Three years ago,*
> *Kelly organized a protest to aid a Colombia tribe whose*
> *sacred lands were being drilled on and exploited by a*
> *large oil company. At the protest her lover Tracy was*
> *raped and killed by guerilla soldiers. Kelly was shot,*
> *thrown off a cliff and left for dead. Elizabeth has just*
> *told Kelly that she blames her for seducing Tracy and*
> *taking her to Colombia to be killed.*

KELLY: I think about killing myself. I think about it a lot.
I'm trying to think of a way to do it. I'm such a baby.
Since getting shot, I can't stand the thought of pain.
You'd think it would toughen me up. Give me some sort
of defense. I was, you know, lying there for something
like twelve hours in pain. The bullet just grazed me, but
the fall shattered the leg bones. And I couldn't think of
anything but the pain. And Tracy. I worried about her
and I cried with pain. That's all I did for twelve hours.
Until the U'wa found me. And since then, if someone
even describes a paper cut to me, I get this reflexive,
sympathetic, paralyzing wave of agony. Sometimes I'll
turn on the TV and there'll be a Western on. And some
Apache warrior will put an arrow through the hero's
side, and I'll just curl up into this whimpering, trembling
ball on the couch and not be able to move. So, I want
to find a way that doesn't hurt. Stupid. I know the pain
wouldn't last more than a minute if I got a gun. Less than
a second. But I think about those twelve hours and there's

just this little crying child inside me. . . . I'm seeing this psychiatrist. My mom set it up. Doesn't help. . . . . And I understand what you feel. About me. About blaming me. I would feel the same. And I'm even grateful for it. If you were one of those women you see on talk shows who go around forgiving the serial child molester who raped and killed their second grader, I wouldn't know what to do. I really think I would probably lose respect for you. I think this way, we're better off. We're on the same page. I understand you. If I were your mom, I'd do the same.

Dramatic
Tracy, early twenties

> *Tracy is a literature major at UCI in her early 20s. She
> is in the dorm room of her friend Kelly. A few days ago
> Tracy had a panic attack while giving a presentation on
> Keats' poem La Belle Dame Sans Merci in a women's
> studies class. Kelly ran after her and talked her out of
> the panic, helping her calm down. Tracy is now tell-
> ing her how grateful she feels and is working up the
> courage to kiss Kelly for the first time.*

TRACY: I think you saved my life or something. I'm a sophomore here. And my whole first year, I spent cowering in
a shower stall because my roommate was gang-banging
entire frat houses in our room. And I spent most of that
time crying. Not because of Lizette, because she probably has every disease known to man, and she'll totally
get hers. And who really cares? But I just hate myself
for not being able to say anything. I never even had it
out with her, you know? I never even said stop it, this
hurts me. Sometimes I'd be too scared to go sit in the
shower stall, and I'd just lie there and listen. Listen to
her and whoever she brought home. And, I've never . . .
you know. I just never did, and this is the first time I'm
hearing some of this stuff. And it's like she's . . . ruining
something for me. Because I don't like it, and it's really
loud, and it just makes me a little sick. And I just die a
little inside, you know? Sometimes it's just disgusting,
and sometimes I'm a little jealous. And I didn't even
switch rooms over Christmas break, because I was worried about hurting her feelings. I was worried about hurting *her* feelings. Isn't that a joke? . . . I'm not strong like
you. You take care of yourself so well, you have enough

left over to go and protect whole South American tribes from throwing themselves off cliffs. You're planning to stop a self-inflicted genocide with just a camcorder and a guy from UC Davis. And I can see you doing it. Putting your own body between those people and the cliffs and making them listen to you. I couldn't even tell my ex-roommate to go screw somewhere else. I don't have that kind of voice. I don't have a voice that can fight, that can plead, that can say something strongly if opposed, that can argue, or that can even disagree. It's like a note I just can't hit. I try and my voice breaks. . . .

(She starts to hyperventilate.)

Sorry. I'm sorry. I wasn't going to go back into class after my panic attack. I was going to leave my purse and everything and just go hide in the toilet. Pull my legs up onto the toilet bowl and hope nobody came looking for me. Because I'm not strong. I'm not strong at all. But you came after me, and we talked. And I just borrowed your strength. I just reached out and borrowed it. I think I pretended I was you. I went back in the room. And you smiled at me and winked. And I had the strength. It probably didn't mean much to you, because I bet you're kind to people and do nice things for them every day. But people haven't been kind to me like that. And I can live off kindness like that a long time. And I did Keats justice. For once I didn't disappoint him. I did his beautiful poem, that piece of poetry I love, some justice.

> *I met a lady in the meads,*
> *Full beautiful - a faery's child,*
> *Her hair was long, her foot was light,*
> *And her eyes were wild.*
> *I made a garland for her head,*
> *And bracelets too, and fragrant zone;*
> *She looked at me as she did love,*
> *And made sweet moan.*

Daniel Guyton

Dramatic
Jess, fifties to sixties

Jess is an older woman in her 50's-60's in an all-female penitentiary, here instructing a younger woman on what to expect from prison.

JESS: Listen, hon. I been here a long time. And I mean a *long* time. I seen a lot of women come and go. A whole lot of women. Some of them friends of mine. Some of them ain't. Some of them left here in a body bag. Some of them walked out on their own recognizance. A few of them went upstate, and I even know six women who went to Federal. Back in the early 90's. But Agnes Ketterman, however? *She* went out through the sewage system, back in '78. About halfway through it, though, she... got stuck. Apparently her leg got jammed up in the filtration unit. Or... so they said. They found pieces of her six weeks later – floating in the Susquehanna River. If you try hard enough here, honey, you can get out. Although you may not look too pretty when you do. I tried escaping once. Back in '79. I didn't get that far though. I bribed one of the guards to look the other way during dinner. He did. But not before telling three other guards to look right at me. I was full of piss and vinegar back in those days, without a goddamn lick of sense in my brain. They waited for me in the freezer, behind the kitchen. Right where I told that son of a bitch I would be. They waited, all bundled up in their warmest winter coats, nicely hidden behind the mashed potatoes, and the baked beans, and the giant cans of sauerkraut. And they watched me yank up that drainage grate, which I had been periodically loosening for over 11 months. Hunh. 11 months. That actually felt like a long time back in those days. But then, just as I removed the grate, they called out to me. One of the guards – Officer… Jettts, or… Betts or something. He said, "Hey Jessie! Say hi to Agnes for me!" Or… something to that effect. I panicked. I tried to squeeze in there as fast as I could, but… the other two grabbed me. It took all three of them to pull me out. They kicked me, tied me up, and then they gang-banged me on the cold freezer floor while everyone else was eatin'. It didn't matter how hard I screamed. Those girls had heard it all before. Since then, I've… heard it many times myself. And that guard I bribed? Officer Hebbard? He just looked away. Just like I paid him to. He kept on looking away. That kind of thing don't… don't offer you much encouragement in the ways of trusting other people, if you know what I mean.

Comic
Priscilla, twenties to forties

> *Priscilla is visiting Joel's hotel room on the last night of a national dating convention for farmers. Joel's grief over his failing dairy farm is holding him back from romance. Priscilla wants to sleep with him before the convention is over and gives him a pep talk.*

PRISCILLA: Jesus Christ could walk in this room right now and not follow what I'm talkin about, does that mean he's not intelligent? No, it means he's from Nazareth and he doesn't have a TV. Take some pride in yourself Joel, think you can tell your children you accomplished... I mean anybody who can keep a farm goin ten, twelve, fifteen years like you've done—and I'm not talkin about my kinda farm in South Carolina where we have TJ Maxx, I'm talkin about your kinda farm. Fourteen cows, that's more than I have anymore. And a hundred years from now when there's an apocalypse and everybody's dyin of cancer from hormones and Monsanto GMO bullshit your great-grandkids'll look up at your picture and say he did things right, that's what kinda people we come from—second of all Joel can I just say somethin, for once? I resent you actin like I'm this normal beauty queen and I've just coasted through life like a debutante. Like granted, you got hang-ups, but my childhood, speakin of cows. Did you see your cousin fuck a cow, Joel? Did you see your cousin fuck a cow? Cause I did. And that was traumatizing. At a formative time in my life. But am I up here bein all sensitive and squirrelly and withholding of sex because of a traumatizing barn incident? No. Never. I would never do that to someone. On her last night of Singles in Agriculture.

For information on this author, click on the
WRITERS tab at www.smithandkraus.com.

Comic
Priscilla, twenties to forties

> *Priscilla is visiting Joel's hotel room on the last night of a national dating convention for farmers. Joel is a Christian fundamentalist with limited sexual experience. In a panic disguised as outrage, he demands to know more about Priscilla's past. She responds by rattling off a list of former lovers.*

PRISCILLA: Okay—okay if it makes you feel better? Mike was my husband, you knew about him. Two, husband of the girl Mike was havin an affair with. And no I didn't love him. And that's when I learned never have sex for the sake of revenge cause I found out later that guy was tied to a straight-up prison gang. Three... okay third guy was Pastor Bill, once. After Mike died. One time. Gah, that man... bless his heart. Fourth guy was a banker I thought was gonna help me with my goats. Did I love him, no. Did I love the idea of that business loan? Probably more than my own mother... Fifth guy was, whatever. My cousin... And he did it with me way before he did it with the cow, those two incidents were unrelated. We were—I was a kid, it was one of those... I mean it was consensual, um. Ronny was just truly a fucked-up person, for him it's a blessing he was born on a farm cause anywhere else he'da been a serial killer. So. But yeah, when I caught him with the cow a couple years later I was like I can't believe I ever slept with that guy. Now he's... man, it's like every fucked-up person I know ends up movin to Florida. Hunh... I mean of course I made him stop, Aunt Rae knew what he was doin too, she was like, "Cilla go check back make sure Ronny's doin okay in the barn." Then sure enough. I was like, "Ronny take your dick outta that cow." I mean I felt bad for the cow, but. Ronny just looked so pathetic and stupid, it almost looked to me like the cow was like laughin at him.

For information on this author, click on the WRITERS tab at www.smithandkraus.com.

Dramatic
Dirdra, thirties

> *Dirdra is speaking to her estranged sister, Janice.
> Dirdra ran away in her teens, leaving Janice alone
> with their crazy mother. They've been reunited for the
> mother's funeral, happy that she's finally dead. Here,
> Dirdra explains why she can't participate in a memorial
> service and how she'd have maternal fantasies about a
> customer at the supermarket deli counter, taking care
> of her children. When she first learned of her mother's
> death, Dirdra got confused, the fantasy became reality
> and she wept for the woman at the deli counter.*

DIRDRA: Hey! I'm here now, and I know what's what and
who's dead, and I'm completely sane and happy. Happy
and sane. So just drop it. *You* do this. Don't act like it's
so…. You do it. You look for them! You look for them.
You do… at the park, on the bus…where ever…. You
know who I'm talking about. You don't wonder... if
somebody took the time to roll up *your* turkey? Zip *your*
zipper up to the neck? It's just us here. You can admit it to
me. I'm not talking about deli meat. I didn't think THAT
mother was MY… That *would* be crazy. I'm way too old
to be her… I mean, she's obviously not my… but if she
was… and if she died, I'd come up with a great memory
about her. The way she rolled up the turkey…like she was
performing surgery. I wouldn't get sick to my stomach
thinking about her. I'd put together a beautiful memorial
service. She'd deserve it. That's not why I cried. I cried
because… as long as mom was alive…there was always
that chance… you know… that hope you hold out even
when you know there's no point... that maybe … I'd wake
up in the morning and she'd be – this is gonna sound

stupid – she'd be… someone else. This stranger in my house would be gone, and my real mother would be there. And my life would finally start. That's how I fell asleep every night in this house… waiting for my real mother. But she's really dead now. She's never gonna turn into someone else at midnight like some fairytale. If I hid it from the world… it's not cuz she wasn't *that* bad… it's cuz it was too awful to admit… even to myself. *(tears up)* I'm not crying. Don't touch me. I'm not giving you a damn hug. I'm not giving you a memory either. Cuz there are none. And stop looking at me like I've got three heads. You're no different than me.

For information on this author, click on the WRITERS tab at www.smithandkraus.com.

Dramatic
Faye, mid-fifties, African American

> *While playing cards in the break room of a stamping plant, Faye tells Dez, a co-worker, how she came to work there. Faye is a determined survivor.*

FAYE: This ain't a democracy. You in my personal breakroom and in the noble effort of thankin' me for not kickin' yo' ass out , you grant me the simple pleasures of playin' a game of cards so that I can graciously and repetitiously take yo' money. You know, you ain't the only in tough shit. When I first come up in this plant, I was pregnant with my first and only. Kinda like Shanita. My son's father ran off and I was assed out. Had dropped outta school to be with him so I ain't have no family to fall back on. My mama didn't play them kinda games. She come from the real ol' school. Once you shame your mama and turn up with a fast tail, you got to be put out and ain't no lookin' back. I was scared shitless but somethin' in me knew I was gonna survive. Not cuz nothin' was promised to me or cuz I could see the light at the end of the tunnel or no shit like that. But somethin' in me knew what I was made of. I was gonna survive cuz I had to. So I walked up, hiding my pregnant belly so I could get me a job, and I got it. Same day. Been workin' the line ever since. Survivin' ever since. And it ain't been no easy work all the time. Even got the battle scars to prove that stamping doors ain't for sissys.

> *(She holds up her arm for Dez to see. A scar skates along her forearm.)*

This beauty right here….From a press machine on 12-line. Years ago. Got backed up and tried to pull the sheet metal that was stuck in the gears. Press came right down by my hand, sparks burned the shit outta me. Coulda been a lot worse if I ain't move my hand quick. That's fast thinkin' like you ain't never seen. But I still got all my limbs. Everything in tact. You know, you really stupid. I'm tellin' you about being pregnant and alone. I'm telling you about having a son and bein' clueless. I'm telling you about not having the answers. Ain't never had 'em and probably never will. But whatever I'm doin', it's keepin' me here. And that's how I can be patient when the plane is headed toward a tree, cuz even if it crash…I don't think I'd die. I think I'd get scarred maybe. But I wouldn't die. Take the train next time. Keep movin'.

For information on this author, click on the
WRITERS tab at www.smithandkraus.com.

Dramatic

Shanita, mid-late twenties, African American

> *Shanita is talking with Faye in the break room of the*
> *stamping plant where they work. Everyone is worried*
> *that the plant might close. Shanita has an opportunity*
> *for another job but she wants to stick it out at the plant*
> *because she loves working there.*

SHANITA: Cassie Logan down on my line got written up yes-
terday for leavin' 2 minutes before her break cuz she had
to pee. Try to tell me I can't break when my baby pressin'
down on my bladder. I don't think so. Some folk say it's
just a scare tactic. Downsizin' and trying to weed out
the people who slackin'. I decided I ain't gonna listen
to all that hearsay. Cuz people gonna end up sabotaging
themselves and get fired....and that ain't gonna be me.
Plus, you our union rep. Everybody know you ain't gonna
take no company shit. Got offered a job over at the Copy
Center on 8 mile. My cousin used to be the manager, but
she movin' offices. Said I could come take over. What I'm
gonna do at a copy center? Day in and day out, runnin'
paper through these simple machines—for what? Don't
got the same kind of pride this work got. Here, I feel
like I'm building somethin' important. Love the way the
line needs me. Like if I step away for even a second and
don't ask somebody to mind my post, the whole operation
has to stop. My touch...my special care....it matter. I'm
building something that you can see come to life at the
end. Got a motor in it and it's gonna take somebody
somewhere. Gonna maybe drive some important business
man to work. Gonna get some single mama to her son's
football practice. Gonna take a family on they first trip
to Cedar Point. Gonna even maybe be somebody's first

time. Who knows? But I like knowing I had a hand in it, you know? That's why I'm gonna turn her down. Don't wanna work at no copy center. What's life at a copy center? Do somethin' I don't believe in? I figure ya'll is right. Time to stop worryin' about something that may not happen. Workin' in this industry is what I do. Uncertainty is always there. But it's the work I'm made of. In me from my daddy. Wanted a son, but got me instead. Always been good with my hands, and this somethin' that makes him proud of me. Not bein' pregnant before I'm married. Not being over twenty-five and building a family by myself. But this? Being a highly skilled job setter…. that's something I can stand on. Everybody can't say that. Everybody can't do what I do. I belong here. Ride it til' the wheels fall off. Right?

For information on this author, click on the WRITERS tab at www.smithandkraus.com.

Seriocomic
Sandy, twenty-eight

> *Sandy is a history teacher at a challenging urban high
> school thinks through her boyfriend's new idea for
> education software, and inspires him with her hopeful
> vision of what it could be.*

SANDY: You know what I'd do in my classroom? What I'd
do, is I'd have, like - let's say two thirds of the class is
kind of getting something. I'd let them use the software,
do the practice problems, have a challenge. And then,
I'd work with the third of the class that wasn't getting it,
and teach like a smaller group lesson. Try a couple different ways of explaining it, have plenty of time to answer
their questions. You create a small class within a big class.
You could do it for the smart kids too. Two thirds of the
class has to practice, but the ones who've been doing
well on the practice questions. You could teach them
something new. Like, special challenge of the week. Or
look at real world applications. Give them an independent
project where they can really direct themselves. And the
weaker students, they'd feel more competent, stay in
school. And what if - what if all of them went out into
the world ready to become primary care physicians!
And medical researchers and environmental engineers
and better teachers and non-stupid congressmen. What if
we actually used all of the potential of every kid coming
out of every public school classroom in America! We'd
have kids ready to take on the environmental crisis!
And the obesity epidemic! And they could *vote* smarter,
because like they understood statistics and economics
and America gets better which means the world gets
better and we save the planet and we don't die in nuclear

war and we grow food in a sustainable manner and we colonize Saturn and spread art and philosophy and hope to the far corners of the universe!

Seriocomic
Photographer, twenties

> *The Photographer has just learned she'll never see
> Lydia again. Lydia's closing her office in the wake of a
> synchronized subway-bombing attack. The two women
> don't know each other, but the Photographer for months
> took daily candid snapshots of Lydia. She was drawn
> to the repetitive monotony of Lydia's life, having had
> very little stability in her own.*

PHOTOGRAPHER: I'm fine. I've just got to get my bearings.
I'm here… with my camera. It's noon, and it's this weird
convergence of the office but not the office, of you but
not you. I hate change. I said that already.

(Tries to collect herself, hits her chest, trying to get air.)

This never would happen with a watermelon or a kiwi
or a pear or even an apple or a raspberry, a strawber-
ry, blueberry, blackberry, honeydew, cantaloupe, papaya,
mango, orange, plum, peach, cherry, pineapple, not even
anything dried: apricots, raisins, craisins, dates, figs. You
must know who I am. You haven't seen the limos? The
celebrities? My studio? One block that way.

(She points.)

The big fruit portraits in the window. I sort of created
a genre. I've been compared to Annie Lebowitz. The
Annie Lebowitz of fruit portraiture. Fruit at its peak is
very powerful. It speaks to people. A perfect moment
in time before it all goes to shit. Fame's fleeting, but
pictures don't change. Not pictures of fruit, anyway.
You were my first human subject. I scoped you out. I
nearly cried when I realized— You were a person. Not a
cumquat. And you were perfect every time. Every time,

the same. In a rut, but in a good way. "Normal." Like a movie: cue the noon bells, cue the lady on the phone, cue the feet on the desk. Even the conversation seemed the same! I had to mark the pictures by date just so I could tell them apart. You were better than fruit. You never changed. Never too green. Never rotten. Day after day. Dependable. I love dependable. It's like… like nine hours of sleep. But today, you're different. AND you're leaving FOREVER!

For information on this author, click on the WRITERS tab at www.smithandkraus.com.

Dramatic
Natalie, twenty-one (if set in college) or seventeen (if set in high school)

> *Natalie didn't expect her evening to turn out like this at all. In preparation for a night of celebration, Natalie got good and drunk, only to find herself brought together with a bunch of other students and presented with a dilemma: one of them has found a video taken at a party that all of them were at, and towards the end of that video is what might be one of their mutual friends, Cal, sexually assaulting a girl not many of them know beyond her reputation: Laura. Natalie, who is still quite inebriated, hasn't said much since this information was revealed, and hasn't said much all night that anybody's taken seriously. But when somebody makes the erroneous assumption that if Laura had been raped, she would have had to have gone to the hospital, Natalie decides to speak up:*

NATALIE: You don't have to go to the hospital. *(beat)* See, I knew a girl this one time who was coming home one night, she was coming home from a bar and, she'd never been to a bar before and, because she was younger than they were, her friends insisted she took a cab home, because they wanted her to be safe, you know, and, so she got to her door and the cab drove away, and at some point in between opening the door and closing the door and the cab driving away, while she was getting the key out for the, um. There was. *(beat)* Anyway, she had this thing happen, where, you know there's this wall on the inside that's a very important wall and when it gets hurt, there's. And there's blood everywhere, sometimes, you know. But. Um. *(beat)* But you know, you don't have to go to the hospital right away if you don't want to. You just got the shit kicked out of you. You don't have to do anything if you don't want to. If you want, you can just sit there. Bleed for a bit, if you're bleeding. Or if you want you can go to the hospital and you can give a fake name or a fake insurance and then when they're not looking, you can leave, but, you don't have to go right away. Not if you don't want to. She hasn't even told her mom yet. *(beat)* What was I saying?

For information on this author, click on the WRITERS tab at www.smithandkraus.com.

Maggie, nineteen-twenty (if set in college) or fifteen-sixteen (if set in high school)

> *Maggie, along with several other students, has been called together to deal with a problem: one of them has found a video taken at a party that all of them were at, and towards the end of that video is what might be one of their mutual friends, Cal, sexually assaulting a girl not many of them know beyond her reputation: Laura. Maggie does know Laura, better than anybody else in this room, and only moments ago, Maggie voted not to take it to the cops. When questioned by her older sister, Maggie reveals that not only was she present when this happened, but that she believes it was consensual. In this speech, Maggie tries to convince these upperclassmen - and herself - that nothing happened.*

MAGGIE: They were leaning up against the island, at first, the table you have in the middle of your kitchen, Sarah? And it was strange, I wasn't used to seeing her like that. Happy. *(Beat.)* She looked so happy. She was so close to him. He had his hand on her arm. We had all split up. Two by two. And every time I looked over, it was a little different. At first, he's making jokes into her ear and she's smiling into her lap and then he's kissing her, you know. He's kissing her. He was holding her. Nobody holds Laura Heller like that. Not ever. Look, you don't know her, but I know her. And watching her like that, it just made me so... happy. We all were. We were together and we started watching and they didn't seem to care, so. It was strange, like, I knew it was strange, but it didn't feel strange, you know? People were smiling, laughing, cheering, even. You know, joke stuff. Egging them on. Telling them to do stuff. But they didn't even notice, so

… I mean, I didn't know that sorta stuff really happened, I mean, not in public, like, I'd never seen anything like that before except like, on the internet but after what happened with Sarah, it didn't seem so strange, you know? I mean, I was embarrassed at first, but that was only because I didn't get what it was yet. Look, I know what it must look like just to see it on a tape, but in reality it wasn't like what you guys think it is. It wasn't violent or scary it was this girl being kissed and loved who never gets kissed or loved and I think Rob was right, you know? I think it might just have been the best night of her life. I mean, it was the best night of mine.

For information on this author, click on the WRITERS tab at www.smithandkraus.com.

Dramatic
Leila, twenties

*Doug, the guy Leila and her boyfriend have invited over
for a threesome, has expressed his insecurity about the
situation. She lays into him.*

LEILA: Is that what therapy encourages these days? Letting
you believe your personal mess is somehow exceptional?
Worthy of all this time and attention? - It's astonishing
the things we're encouraged to obsess over. Doug: I don't
mean to sound harsh, but I don't care. If your therapist
is giving you confidence, then I guess you're getting
your money's worth. But I would get him to advise
you to know when to stop talking, because that's what
prevents you from closing the deal. And then, on top of
all this, you want me to pander to your insecurities? You
want me to what, tell you how manly you are? You want
me to be a mommy for you and give you confidence? Oh,
that's right, you told us mommy was a monster. Great,
you're turning me into your mother. Why is it that men
always want us to be nurses to their fragile egos? Isn't it
enough what we do? Now we're responsible for making
you feel like a man? Because God forbid you should feel
anything less? No, Doug. I don't want to sleep with
you. Even theoretically. I'm sorry if I'm adding to your
insecurities, and I know I'm supposed to be nurturing,
but I have to tell you, I'm all nurtured-out at the moment.
I barely have enough for myself.

Dramatic
Clara, early thirties

Clara is pacing the living room, speaking on her cell phone.

CLARA: And she really did it. She fucking burnt them! ...
Yeah, the apartment smells like hell, or the other way
around... It doesn't matter now! She's my sister, my own
fucking sister... I was adopted from Karvystan. I called mom
and she confirmed. Then she made an appointment to her
shrink... How can you ask that? Of course she's staying
here. She's my SISTER!... I don't know about tomorrow,
I can't think about that right now - I still have a grenade
on my table... Ok, Ok, don't panic, I will get rid of that
grenade... She's sleeping in the bedroom, she must be exhausted, poor thing, to burn all those, all my—Anyway, to
hell with the past, we must live in the present... I asked her
to be my bridesmaid!... She didn't say 'yes', but she didn't
say 'no' either... Look, honey, I gotta go now, I must wake
her up, she's invited to this dinner reception tonight, she's
gonna talk about—... yes, of course I'm going with her,
she's my rock star sister!... Oh, and guess what! The guy
from Rutgers called. He wanted to make sure they're still on
with my book... they heard I was interviewing her... This
whole thing is—I'm totally psyched!... My life has turned
upside down in one crazy day... Yeah, I'm OK, I'm fucking
great! ... I'm not shouting! This is the Karvystanian way of
talking when someone is excited!

(She jumps around.)

Yeah, I'm kinda dancing. Actually jumping from one
red horse on my carpet to another... Of course they
are red horses! Red WILD horses. Karvystanian horses,
honey. Get used to that.

Comic
Trish, forty

> *Trish is talking to a new friend, Jan. Jan thinks that she*
> *is totally uncool and envies Trish. Trish explains that*
> *she was actually not cool at first and that Jan can be*
> *cool by being herself.*

TRISH: I wore dolly lace shirts in college. Carried a designer
purse. Drove Mommy and Daddy's BMW. Straightened
my straight hair to make it extra 35 straight. I was the first
sophomore to be elected SGA Vice President. No dates.
Not. Cool. Yeah. Big time bummer. And all that time, all
the SGA success, designer whatever, didn't bring me any
happiness. I was on the longest, loneliest road of my life.
But then I got invited to this party. In a big barn of the
student council president. A sophomore at a senior class
party. And this girl from school was there. I'd wanted to
be her best friend forever. She was cool. Leather jacket
cool, ya' know? Rizzo cool. Without the abortion stuff
but, like, Sandy cool at the end of the movie. As cool as
Rhonda. *(a quick beat)* And this girl, this Rizzo, she's
always the life of the party. And I wanted to prove to her
that I could be too. But I couldn't even get the nerve to
go up and sit near her, you know, I couldn't even, I mean,
I had been invited. Someone clearly thought that I was
cool enough to be at this party. But the problem was I
didn't think that I was cool enough. So I had a couple of
shots. And then a couple of bottles of Goldschlager Pep-
permint Schnapps, and ended up... I fucked a chicken. I
mean, I didn't really have sex with it. I mean, not having anything to stick into its'... but I masturbated on,
pretended to masturbate on, because Rizzo, she was
making jokes about this cow, this cow that the guys

were going up to, pulling their dicks out and pretending to fuck. And Rizzo was laughing her ass off, giving them high fives, so I just thought, you know, I could get in on that. This way, she'll think I'm cool. She'll high five me and ask me to sit next to her, you know, best friend stuff. So I grabbed a chicken and pulled my jeans and panties down to my knees and just sorta' rubbed it around. But then, everybody, just stopped laughing. Rizzo step towards me, and puked whiskey and rye all over me and the chicken. And I was just standing there, covered in vomit and feathers, holding this squawking… I ran away the next day. I couldn't go back to school, go back, anywhere. My mom and dad heard about it all. Disowned me. A couple days later I was hitchhiking and got picked up by a Whitesnake roadie and that was that. 20 years later, and here I be.

For information on this author, click on the WRITERS tab at www.smithandkraus.com.

THE TRIUMPHANT RETURN OF BLACKBIRD FLYNT

Peter Ullian

Dramatic
Lady Jane, early to mid-twenties

> *Lady Jane, the child of sixties radicals hiding out from the FBI, was a teen-age runaway and drug addict until she joined a commune and got herself clean. That's where she met Blackbird Flynt, who recruited her to join his band of would-be revolutionaries dedicated to overthrowing the government of mid-1980s America. After a failed back robbery, however, the surviving members of the band reconnoiter back at their hide-out, not sure if their leader is alive or dead. Thompson, one of the younger members, decides he's going back to the bank to finish the job — alone. Lady Jane tries to convince him this would a suicide mission – and a very bad idea.*

LADY JANE: Don't try to be a martyr, Thompson. Christ, if you have to kill yourself, don't go to all this trouble! Just pick up this gun and put a bullet through your thick skull! It's so much easier! Really, it's very, very easy. Just blast a hole through your head. In one side and out the other. Shoot your brains out all over the wall. We'll clean it up. Don't worry. Go ahead. If that's what you want, go ahead and do it! After the mess we've seen at the bank, why do you want to go back and make another one? I'll tell you what's going to happen, Thompson. I'll tell you exactly what's going to happen. You are going to walk in through the door and you are going to feel a bullet rip through your right arm. And it is going to feel like fire. And then you are going to feel the same thing in you left arm. And you will look at your arms, and you will see blood and bone and muscle and flesh hanging out of the holes in your sleeves. And then you are going to catch one in the gut, and it is going to hurt like nothing you have ever felt before. And then you are going to feel your leg, your whole right leg get shot out from under you by a shotgun blast and go flying across the room. And you will go down. You will be on one knee and one stub. And all you will see is the floor, and the pool of blood, getting wider and wider. Your blood. Your own crimson, scarlet, all-American, ruby-red blood. And you won't be able to move, because every muscle in your body has a bullet lodged inside of it. You won't be able to breathe, because there will be bullets in both of your lungs. And then an F.B.I. man in a brown suit and dark glasses is going to walk up to you, put a pistol to the back of your neck, and blow your moronic brains out all over the floor.

For information on this author, click on the WRITERS tab at www.smithandkraus.com.

Dramatic
Ellie, twenties - forties

*Ellie tells her good friend Diana that she is fearful that
the dreams she once had will not come true.*

ELLIE: Oh, gee! I should be more like you, right Diane? Is
that what you're saying? I should go around asking guys
out? And it shouldn't matter if I get shot down. Fuck the
pain! As long as I feel! As long as I feel something! And
I should go around and jump into the sack with anyone
who wags their dick at me. So I can feel! So I can be
like you! "Hi. I'm Diane. Everything is fine. My life
is great. The world is a perfect place to live. And I'm
destined to live happily ever after." Fuck happily ever
after! Whoever coined that expression should be shot!
Who lives happily ever after?! Who?! Only morons
live happily ever after. I can't but into that. I just can't.
It's a myth that's not going to happen to me! You get it,
Diane?! It's not going to happen to me! *(pause)* I had
dreams growing up. Big dreams. And my dreams were
probably not all that different than yours. All I wanted
was to live "happily ever after." And my "happily ever
after" dreams always included a mate. A man. We'd fall
in love. We'd be husband and wife. And that union would
bring dividends, a child. Actually, in my "happily ever
after dreams," children. We'd be a family. And we'd live
in a house. And have a great backyard. And a swing set.
And a gazebo. *(There was always a fuckin' gazebo in
my dream.)* And this man and I would be parents. And
we'd watch our children grow up. And we'd attend P.T.A.
meetings. And we'd grow old together. And IT'S NOT
HAPPENING!! Do you hear me, Diane?! IT'S NOT

HAPPENING!! What happens to dreams, Diane? Tell me! You seem to know everything. Do they change? Do we get to keep changing our dreams when we realize they're not happening.? Do they dry up and disappear? Are dreams matter? Can they be created and destroyed? Do dreams matter? Do we get a certain amount of dreams in our lifetime? Do I only get a certain amount, like my eggs? And every time I bleed I have less and less and less until I won't bleed anymore?! I won't have to bleed anymore because all my dreams will be gone?! Is that what happens to dreams? Do they bleed out of you until there are none left? Tell me, dammit! I want to go into a movie theater, sit down, and tell all the other people that come in, all the other people in the world, in the universe, that the seat next to me is saved! "Oh, here he is. Here's the guy I'm saving it for. The guy bringing me popcorn." I WANT POPCORN!! I WANT POPCORN!! I WANT POPCORN!!

(She breaks down and begins to cry. A beat.)

What will happen to me if I can't dream anymore? Will I die?

Seriocomic
Ellie, twenties - forties

Ellie is trying her best to get in shape.

ELLIE: I go to the gym to work out. I do. Really. But even I
have to admit it. I go there to socialize too. I mean, it's not
like I'm the Rapmaster trying to make it with every guy I
see. I'm more discerning than that. I mean, guys are like
Chinese restaurants, there are good ones and there are bad
ones, and all the menus are pretty much the same. And
they all think their Moo Shoo Pork is the best. I mean,
there are some guys who go to the club for a good reason:
it gets their heads out of their refrigerators for an hour. I
personally think the club should have a rule prohibiting
those guys from wearing Spandex. But, it's cool. I give
those guys a lot of credit for trying to uncover the Adonis
living inside them. Then there are the guys who are on
the maintenance program keeping their perfect bodies
perfect. Those are the guys who drive me crazy. They're
all gay. Hey, what can I say? There's something about
watching a guy work out that really turns me on. They
sit in the seat and strap themselves in with this big leather
belt. They're surrounded by metal and steel. And they
pump! Hard! They sweat! They pump and they throb.
They pump and they pulsate. They're dripping, dripping,
dripping...man, if there's a better turn on than watching a
guy work up a good sweat, I' like to know about it. But
I do go to the club to work out. I do. Hey, check it out...

(She displays her biceps.)

Arms like bombs! *(pause)* And if I guy gets turned on
by watching me work out, watching me drip, so much
the better. I mean, why not, right? It's there, so you look.
What? You're not going to look? C'mon...you gotta look.

Dramatic
Mondo, early fifties

> *Embroiled in a bitter divorce and suffering from a stress-induced eye disorder, Mondo has just been advised against a laser surgery that would resolve her eye condition in time for her next court appearance. She's worried about having to represent herself in court, especially with instability and discomfort associated with her compromised eye. She speaks to the audience.*

MONDO: When you deal with the legal system it's scary, folks. Because you realize there is no justice there. You're right, but you cannot prove anything. We agreed before the court that I would keep the house. I offered to pay him $6,000, he says it's worth more money, it's close to a historical district. Vinyl siding. You can hear it flapping. It's like living in a tree. They're not gonna put it in the historic book, our house. He wants 8,000. Oh gosh. So I wrote him a check $8,000, so it's out of my way. Then he says in court, listen now, he's with someone else, he says he has the kind of wife who doesn't support him. Judge told me to say something, I told the Judge, horrible macho judge, Wilbur Smith. I told him, I don't confess to know the law, but I couldn't afford to have a lawyer, that's why I was myself . My husband's lawyer said my husband was victim. I start to talk, Judge made faces. With me he made face, he didn't listen. But he listened to my husband. If I argued the way he did, I'd be in prison. My husband said he asked for his wife to help him and I didn't. I said, yes I did, I gave a check for the house. He looked at me in the eyes and said he never saw the check. That dropped the cake. The Judge was about to call someone to find out if he ever got the check, and my husband says, "I think I remember I received something." He lied! In court! Because he lied, I kept my house, folks. But he had another house, besides the one we lived. On the top of everything, he's a junk collector. He was possessed of the junk collecting. He had fines from the other house from codes. The house is like a garage, a three floor garage with stuff. Walls needed to be demolished, fence, it was a danger for kids. Judge ruled I have ten weeks to clean the house or go to jail. Me. Stuff was his stuff. Expected me to do all this when it was his stuff. I was responsible for his stuff. So chauvinistic pig. It was like I was on the 14th century. I was so surprised I didn't see any guillotines to decapitate women if they said no.

For information on this author, click on the WRITERS tab at www.smithandkraus.com.

Dramatic
Mondo, early fifties

> *Over the course of her divorce proceedings, Mondo*
> *receives a court order to clear out a junk-filled stor-*
> *age facility maintained by her soon-to-be ex-husband.*
> *While attempting to dispose of a lifetime's accumula-*
> *tion of someone else's junk, she speaks to the audience.*

MONDO: He didn't discriminate against junk. Driving
around sees plastic, he picks it up. How much junk, you
can't imagine, folks. Sees a plastic flower on the street,
he picks it up. He wanted me to put a "Baby on Board" in
my car because he picked it up somewhere! I don't have a
baby! He had this mentality of people who are alcoholic.
Driving, next block, there is trash there, he takes it. He
saw something, he said, this is brand new. He picked up
computers. Going here and there to find stuff, in case
he needs. Everything and anything and everywhere! "I
can use this to make business." He was gonna fix it and
sell it. He never sold a thing. (*pause*) First time I realized how junky he was: I came to his house. Car was
junky, he said how good car was. He has this junk car,
big car full of painting. I said what are you gonna do with
all this? He said, "We just got house, we can use painting." Right. "I bought all this for nothing, only $100." We
had to carry it to the house, 2 gallons, 1 gallon, all day
carrying the painting. So much painting, we could paint
the whole neighborhood, folks! We gave some to a couple
friends, they brought it back, said it was no good. That's
why the store was giving it away, it was no good! Where
can you use this stuff? (*pause*) We had a friend in Philly
who worked next to the river and a flood took his car. He
was going to give away his car for free. We call the guy,

my husband starts asking questions, "What's the problem with the car?" He goes on, problems, problems, the car didn't work! "Does the door open?" "No." "Does the window open?" "No." "Can you turn it on?" "No." He kept asking questions. Nothing you could say would make him not want this car! Can't put on A/C cause the car stinks. He says, "Maybe I can take it to a place, and I can clean it." He had to have that car. Like he had to have everything. (*pause*) Betrayal means shit. Betrayal means you were an idiot and you feel sorry for yourself. Forget the word betrayal. There was no betrayal, he was just doing what he always did, collecting. Of course he would pick up a girlfriend, he picked up everything. You can never have enough junk, folks.

For information on this author, click on the WRITERS tab at www.smithandkraus.com.

Dramatic
Mondo, early fifties

> *At her last visit with her eye doctor Mondo struggles*
> *to keep her composure as she learns her recovery has*
> *reached a plateau. If her eye doesn't significantly im-*
> *prove soon, she'll need to undergo a risky surgery. She*
> *speaks to the audience.*

MONDO: Crap, folks. I didn't wanna cry in front of him, but lately I'm the crying baby. I'm crying, I never pretend I live to the fullest. I got something from my mom that's difficult to inherit. Not money. To be brave. Spirit. Never my parents say the most important thing is to be happy. Say, when I got married, say: you no longer exist. (*pause*) Most females embedded in society we invest so much in the relationship. Even the high-educated, high-intelligent women. I know people change, grow, not always the direction you like. And men fool around. They love you. But they love ten other women. (*pause*) My friend Melpomeni found Yianni Malakas on the computer and said, "OMIGOD" She moved to Oregon for his job. She wasn't doing anything of substance. That becomes baby and husband. I wouldn't wanna be an ant in her shoes. She's the only one I could stand from the Greek community. As the bell rings seven o'clock they're in church. Say all crap about God, I don't give a damn about God. I don't need any freak around me to make me feel edgy. Something happened to me, I called my husband. I used to come home, ask how was your day. Now come home and I am myself. Eat myself. Sleep myself. Be alone. Something happens to me, I don't call anybody. (*pause*) I didn't like who my husband changed into be, so I'm disappointed at him. But we had chemistry.

We are so differently intellectually and life orientation, but we had chemistry, and I could have tried. I rushed to the divorce and now all the good times are dead. It hits you. It might hit you the day, or tomorrow but when it comes, it's such a tear-jerking shit. (*pause*) My husband was part of my Greek identity. Now my Greek period is over. I need to lose some part of my character, what I carry culturally. It has to be, everything has been destroyed for me as far as Greek. I need to integrate, involve more. Embrace more America.

For information on this author, click on the WRITERS tab at www.smithandkraus.com.

Dramatic
D, thirties

> *D, who is in the middle of editing a film, gives a lecture*
> *after learning the stars (her boyfriend and the writer's*
> *wife) were having an affair during its filming.*

D: The temptation... is to leave your mark. Initials under the seat. A flaw in the rug. Something, anything, that says, "I was here. I existed." We must resist that temptation. We are magicians, but our trick is to be invisible. Our calling card must be blank. No one can ever think of us. If they do, something is very, very wrong. They say a film is born three times: once when it's written, once again when it's shot, and once, finally, when it's edited. Sometimes, the first two births go well, and your birth... is a painless one. It's like a dream. Everything makes sense. The way forward is as simple and perfect as a straight, black line. All you have to do is follow it faithfully, to the end. But often, the first two births are *not* easy births. There are complications. Things go wrong. Moments are lost. Mistakes are made. What looked good on the page often is not. What felt great on the day often was not. *We* are left with the pieces. Both the ones we have and the ones we don't, the ones that are missing. All we have is what we are given. We can make nothing, we can create nothing. We can only interpret, suggest associations, by proximity, in the hope that... something might be understood. We are not weavers, we are quilt-makers. We are scavengers, searching through the rubble, sorting through the mess. To use that which appears unusable. To save that which appears unsalvageable. To make sense... of the senseless. Sometimes this can be difficult. Sometimes, almost impossible. And *sometimes*... it *is* impossible.

Sometimes the mess wins. And no one knows why. Everyone tried. Everyone did their best. But, in the end, it's still a mess. It's not your fault. You're just the one left sitting in it. *It is not your fault.* There'll be another one. Sometimes you won't *want* there to be another one... But there will be. And if you're lucky, it'll be better. And if you're *really* lucky... it'll be amazing. But you know what? Even if it is amazing. It's still a mess. That's what they don't tell you. It's all just a mess, the whole thing. Even on the good days, it's a sort of... nightmare that you have to live inside. That you have to learn. Every foot. Every frame. Until you know it by heart. Until you see it when you close your eyes at night. Until you really do dream it. And then waking up. Trying to make it better. Trying to make it perfect. And failing. Endlessly... endlessly failing. The whole thing's a nightmare.

Dramatic
Sabrina, thirty-eight

> *It's 1978 and Sabrina's brother, Kirk, died 10 years ago
> in the Vietnam War. She and her brother were adopted
> by a Mexican-American woman, Carmen. Sabrina ad-
> dresses Carmen.*

SABRINA: Kirk is your habit. Your compulsion. You need him like heroin needs a junkie. I'm a cute little extra that came along for the ride. It's hard to really love a person, isn't it? It requires all sorts of pesky feelings that creep up from the inside out. You think I block him out when I really rush him in. He is water. Omnipresent. The demigod of my life. You want me to bury him alongside your imaginary placenta? You want me to bury him in my imagination? Is that your plan? I've got to go, you know. I've got to work. In California. And it's a big job. Lots of hours. And cubicles. And phone systems. People need to be transferred and get their calls. It's really complicated to keep the whole work thing afloat. It takes all of my concentration. And all of my time. I have to keep my focus over there or things will fall apart. I have to keep myself from sinking. Below. Below. Got to stay up, Carmen. Got to stay away from the scary stuff, you know, because. And that's why. That's why it's hard to go there. Because. Because.

Seriocomic
Whitney, thirties

> *Whitney is participating in a clinical trial of a new medication for schizoid personality disorder. She is speaking to Max, another participant, who has asked her about her fantasy world.*

WHITNEY: This is so hard. How do you describe a world? It isn't a story with a beginning, middle and end. It's a world. I'll start with the earliest world stories from when I was in junior high, and the world first coalesced into a coordinated whole. The torture and execution of Marvina of Taurus Seven! Marvina was a space pirate and a princess and a water-breathing amphibious archeologist. Okay, that's a little unrealistic, sure. But I was twelve when I first made her up. She went on a quest to find the ruins of an underwater alien city to retrieve an artifact that would save humanity from being enslaved by robots this one time. And she met and fell in love with the high priest of a dark cult of demon-worshipping opera singers. And they had three sons. Mikor, Sebastian and Dorrick. Marvina found the artifact and saved humanity and settled down to raise the boys as a single mother. Only this other cult — a demon-worshipping rival cult of belly dancers — wanted to kill her sons. So she killed the belly dancing cult leader and got arrested by the planetary governing council headed by Vernonian the Cursegiver. And it shouldn't have been a big deal because it was in self-defense. But Vernonian used the arrest as an excuse to put Marvina into a trial of mortal combat with a special executioner android trained to torture and kill amphibious races in a water arena- Glibtrar Drathmek! And so Marvina got thrown into this water arena to fight Glibtrar to the death. And it was televised and her sons watched as she was tortured and murdered. And there was nothing they could do. So, from there, my fantasy world branched off into three different stories of personal vengeance. Because Mikor, Sebastian and Dorrick were sent in disguise to three different colony worlds out of fear that Vernonian, having killed their mother would come after them next. Do you want to hear about Mikor, Sebastian or Dorrick next?

Dramatic
Whitney, thirties

> *Whitney and Max are participants in a clinical trial*
> *for a new drug to cure schizoid personality disorder.*
> *Max has told Whitney about a dark hole in his fantasy*
> *world where they put women, which is a constant tor-*
> *ment to him. Whitney has a solution to cure this tor-*
> *ment. Mikor and Selestina are characters in Whitney's*
> *fantasy world.*

WHITNEY: *Put me in the hole!* Make the woman in the hole
me! I know you don't normally pick who goes in— but
try really hard to make it me. It's perfect, Max! Think
about it. You know I'm smart and manipulative and I
would figure out how to get out, kill the serial killer and
get to a police station eventually. And the me inside the
hole won't have access to the pills. I won't have my world
in the real world, but the me in the hole will still have my
whole world! It will live on secretly inside of your world.
And the me in the hole won't even mind living in a hole.
She'll just curl up happily on the cot and think about her
world. Maybe she'll even think out loud and you can
tell me what Mikor and Selestina are doing. It's perfect.
Please. *It's the best of both worlds!* Literally! We get to
keep both our worlds. And I'll take really good care of
you. I'll make you lie down and try to sleep every night.
And drink and eat at least twice a day. And the me in the
hole won't be scared and won't make you worried. I
know that the me in the hole will eventually get that
door open! And she'll find the police and then you'll
have a whole team of police officers in the hole and your
world will get bigger! You'll find out whether there is a
ladder or stairs outside the door. And where the bunker

is— I think it is probably in a remote, isolated state park. In Montana or Wyoming maybe. Me in the hole will find out. You already let me into your world once. When we shared them. I know it feels invasive to have someone else in your world. But try to stay neutral even if you aren't accepting yet. And let me convince you. I'll survive. I'll get out.

Seriocomic
Mae, thirty-two

> *Mae is home taking care of her dad who has a rare,*
> *aggressive form of cancer. Horny and desperate for a*
> *little alone time, she sneaks out to Hank's Saloon – a*
> *local dive bar. There she meets Mac, with whom she*
> *supposedly went to high school. Mac confesses he's*
> *been secretly in love with Mae since the 4th grade. Mae*
> *is having a hard time remembering Mac. It's start-and-*
> *stop at first but then the conversation flows.*

MAE: I used to have a fantasy where my high school boyfriend Dave Gallightly – who totally cheated on me and
like destroyed all of my self-confidence – would come
to my window and knock on my window and then I
would let him in and then he would be high on cocaine
(even though I'm pretty sure he never did cocaine) and
he would like rape me? And the whole time I'm thinking: Maybe I should scream! If I scream, my parents
will wake up and come down here and save me and this
whole thing will stop. But then if my parents come down
here, they'll see me naked with Dave on top of me. And
I'm like a virgin. And super Christian. So I don't scream.
Because I'm too embarrassed. And he rapes me. And then
later I decide to report it. And the whole town vilifies me
and I'm like this outcast woman? And then Dave dies in
a drunk driving accident and everyone is like: If you had
just not reported it he would have died anyway and you
would've gotten justice without having to besmirch his
name. *(Beat.)* I guess that's not really a fantasy. I guess
I just used to think about it when I needed to cry.

Dramatic
Mae, 32

> *Mae is back in Minneapolis after a rough several months. She lost her job, ended her longterm relationship, and went home to help take care of her dad during his cancer treatments. She's been stressed out and down-in-the-dumps for so long that happiness sneaks up on her.*

MAE: I'm out walking. Further than I've walked in months. And the whole world is cold and white but the cold feels kind of good on my face and I feel warm in my coat and I keep walking all the way from my apartment to downtown Minneapolis until my feet get cold and wet with sweat and I duck into a Trailblazer looking for some boots. All the snow boots in all the world are sold-out online. I'm not joking. This is not a joke. They are actually sold-out because people are freaking out about the Polar Vortex. So I'm not particularly hopeful when I duck into this Trailblazer but there's a man there holding a box of insoles and he says they have one pair left. Sorels. "What size are you?" "I'm a size seven." "Shoot. These are sixes." But I try them on anyway and they fit! "Sorels run big," I tell him. *(His name is Eric.)* "They're not making any more this season," Eric says. "That's crazy! They're all sold out!" "You better be careful walking home. People are going to try to steal those boots from you." And Eric calls me "the luckiest girl in all of Minneapolis." And I walk home hugging those boots to my chest. In the elevator of my building an old lady is talking to the doorman. He shouts at her, "Pea soup is better! I want pea soup!" "Sure thing, Bob. I've just gotta get some– "Hambone." She turns to me, explaining, "I've known Bob for 25 years. We make things for each other. It's cool." It *is* cool. "That's what friends are for!" And I go into my apartment. And I put on my boots. And I think about what I want to eat for dinner. And I start to feel something that I haven't felt in a while. In a long while. What is this feeling Happiness. For no reason at all. Just happiness. Just standing in my living room wearing boots. Just full of happiness. For no reason. Just standing in my boots. All alone.

AIRLINE HIGHWAY © 2014 by Lisa D'Amour. Reprinted by permission of Antje Oegel, AO International. For performance rights, contact Antje Oegel (aoegel@ aoegelinternational.com)

A TO Z © 2015 by Monica Raymond. Reprinted by permission of Monica Raymond. For performance rights, contact Monica Raymond (femmevox@hotmail.com)

BARBECUE © 2015 by Robert O'Hara. Reprinted by permission of Ron Gwiazda, Abrams Artists. For performance rights, contact Ron Gwiazda (ron.gwiazda@ abramsartny.com)

BARRIER ISLANDS © 2015 by Lizzie Vieh. Reprinted by permission of Lizzie Vieh. For performance rights, contact Lizzie Vieh (elizabethrvieh@gmail.com)

BLOOMSDAY © 2014 by Steven Dietz. Reprinted by permission of Beth Blickers, Agency for the Performing Arts. For performance rights, contact Beth Blickers (bblickers@apa-agency.com)

BONNIE'S FUTURE SISTERS © 2014 by Meghan Gambling. Reprinted by permission of Meghan Gambling. For performance rights, contact Meghan Gambling (meggamster@gmail.com)

COMPOSURE © 2015 by Scott Sickles. Reprinted by permission of Barbara Hogenson, Barbara Hogenson Agency. For performance rights, contact Barbara Hogenson (bhogenson@aol.com)

THE CUBAN SPRING © 2013 by Vanessa Garcia. Reprinted by permission of Vanessa Garcia. For performance rights, contact Vanessa Garcia (vgarcia43@yahoo.com)

CUDDLES © 2013 by Joseph Wilde. Reprinted by permission of Matt Connell, Berlin Associates. For performance rights, contact Matt Connell (matt@berlinassociates.com)

DEVIL DOG SIX © 2016 by Fengar Gael. Reprinted by permission of Alexis Williams, Bret Adams Ltd. For performance rights, contact Alexis Williams (awilliams@ bretadamsltd.net)

DOSTOYEVSKI © 2015 by Don Nigro. Reprinted by permission of Don Nigro. For performance rights, contact Samuel French, Inc., 212-206-8990, www.samuelfrench.com

DOT © 2015 by Colman Domingo. Reprinted by permission of Kate Navin, Gersh Agency. For performance rights, contact Kate Navin (knavin@gershny.com)

DRINK ME © 2011 by Fengar Gael. Reprinted by permission of Alexis Williams, Bret Adams Ltd. For performance rights, contact Alexis Williams (awilliams@bretadamsltd.net)

EYES SHUT. DOOR OPEN © 2015 by Cassie M. Seinuk. Reprinted by permission of Cassie M. Seinuk. For performance rights, contact Cassie M. Seinuk (cmseinuk@ gmail.com)

FADE © 2015 by Tanya Saracho. Reprinted by permission of Mark Orsini, Bret Adams Ltd. For performance rights, contact Mark Orsini (morsini@bretadamsltd.net)

FANTASIA DECOLORES © 2015 by Maura Campbell. Reprinted by permission of Maura Campbell. For performance rights, contact Maura Campbell (mauracampbell22@gmail.com)

FISH EYE © 2011 by Lucas Kavner. Reprinted by permission of Jared Weber, ICM Partners. For performance rights, contact Di Glazer (dglazer@icmpartners.com)

THE GODDESS OF MURDEROUS RAIN (3) © 2015 by Don Nigro. Reprinted by permission of Don Nigro. For performance rights, contact Samuel French, Inc., 212-206-8990, www.samuelfrench.com

THE GOLDILOCKS ZONE © 2016 by Ian August. Reprinted by permission of Ian August. For performance rights, contact Ian August (ijaugust@hotmail.com)

THE GOODBYE LETTERS © 2015 by Sam Bobrick. Reprinted by permission of Ron Gwiazda, Abrams Artists. For performance rights, contact Ron Gwiazda (ron. gwiazda@abramsartny.com)

THE GRASS IS GREENEST AT THE HOUSTON ASTRODOME © 2014 by Michael Ross Albert. Reprinted by permission of Michael Ross Albert. For performance rights, contact Michael Ross Albert (info@michaelrossalbert.com)

GRAVEYARD OF EMPIRES © 2015 by Elaine Romero. Reprinted by permission of Alexis Williams/Bruce Ostler, Bret Adams Ltd.. For performance rights, contact Alexis Williams (awilliams@bretadamsltd.net) or Bruce Ostler (bostler@bretadamsltd.net)

HAPPILY EVER AFTER © 2015 by Mark Dunn. Reprinted by permission of Mark Dunn. For performance rights, contact Mark Dunn (montydunn@comcast.net)

HIRED EXPECTATIONS © 2015 by Steve Shade. Reprinted by permission of Steve Shade. For performance rights, contact Steve Shade (sgrshade@aol.com)

I AM NOT AN ALLEGORY © 2015 by Libby Emmons. Reprinted by permission of Libby Emmons. For performance rights, contact Libby Emmons (li88yemmons@ gmail.com)

INFORMED CONSENT © 2014 by Deborah Zoe Laufer. Reprinted by permission of Deborah Zoe Laufer. For performance rights, contact Derek Zasky, William Morris Endeavor (dsz@wmeentertainment.com)

INLAND EMPRESS © 2016 by Tom Cavanaugh. Reprinted by permission of Tom Cavanaugh. For performance rights, contact Tom Cavanaugh (tcavana136@aol.com)

IT'S ALL ABOUT LORRIE © 2016 by Joseph Krawczyk. Reprinted by permission of Joseph Krawczyk. For performance rights, contact Joseph Krawczyk (krawjay@ gmail.com)

PERILS OF HUMAN DISCOURSE © 2015 by Sonia Sobieski. Reprinted by permission of Sonia Sobieski. For performance rights, contact Sonia Sobieski (sonyasobieski@yahoo.com)

RIGHT BRUTAL © 2015 by Max Baker. Reprinted by permission of Max Baker. For performance rights, contact Max Baker (mpbbaker@gmail.com)

SAY HI TO AGNES FOR ME © 2015 by Daniel Guyton. Reprinted by permission of Daniel Guyton. For performance rights, contact Daniel Guyton (dguyton21@gmail.com)

SANS MERCI © 2015 by Johnna Adams. Reprinted by permission of Alexis Williams/Bruce Ostler, Bret Adams Ltd.. For performance rights, contact Alexis Wiliiams (awilliams@bretadamsltd.net) or Bruce Ostler (bostler@bretadamsltd.net)

SINGLES IN AGRICULTURE © 2015 by Abby Rosebrock. Reprinted by permission of Abby Rosebrock. For performance rights, contact Abby Rosebrock (m.abigail.rosebrock@gmail.com)

SISTER SISTER © 2016 by Barbara Blumenthal-Ehrlich. Reprinted by permission of Barbara Blumenthal-Ehrlich. For performance rights, contact Barbara Blumenthal-Ehrlich (barbarablumenthalehrliich@gmail.com)

SKELETON CREW © 2015 by Dominique Morisseau. Reprinted by permission of Jonathan Mills, Paradigm Agency. For performance rights, contact Jonathan Mills (jmills@paradigmagency.com)

START DOWN © 2015 by Eleanor Burgess. Reprinted by permission of Alexis Williams, Bret Adams Ltd. For performance rights, contact Alexis Williams (awilliams@bretadamsltd.net)

STILL LIFE © 2015 by Barbara Blumenthal-Ehrlich. Reprinted by permission of Barbara Blumenthal-Ehrlich. For performance rights, contact Barbara Blumenthal-Ehrlich (barbaretc@aol.com)

STUDENT BODY © 2015 by Frank Winters. Reprinted by permission of Jared Weber, ICM Partners. For performance rights, contact Di Glazer, ICM Partners (dglazer@icmpartners.com)

THREESOME © 2015 by Yussef El Guindi. Reprinted by permission of Leah Hamos, Gersh Agency. For performance rights, contact Leah Hamos (lhamos@gershny.com)

TOYS © 2015 by Saviana Stanescu. Reprinted by permission of Saviana Stanescu. For performance rights, contact Saviana Stanescu (savianas@yahoo.com)

TRISH TINKLER GETS SAVED © 2015 by Jacqueline Goldfinger. Reprinted by permission of Amy Wagner, Abrams Artists. For performance rights, contact Amy Wagner (amy.wagner@abramsartny.com)

THE TRIUMPHANT RETURN OF BLACKBIRD FLYNT © 2015 by Peter Ullian. Reprinted by permission of Susan Gurman, Susan Gurman Agency, LLC. For performance rights, contact Broadway Play Publishing, 212-772-8334, www.broadwayplaypubl.com

TWO-PIECE © 2015 by Gary Richards. Reprinted by permission of Gary Richards. For performance rights, contact Gary Richards (grichardsnyc@aol.com)

WIDE AWAKE HEARTS © 2016 by Brendan Gall. Reprinted by permission of Brendan Gall. For performance rights, contact Brendan Gall (gallbrendan@gmail.com)

A WORK OF ART © 2015 by Elaine Romero. Reprinted by permission of Alexis Williams/Bruce Ostler, Bret Adams Ltd.. For performance rights, contact Alexis Williams (awilliams@bretadamsltd.net) or Bruce Ostler (bostler@bretadamsltd.net)

WORLD BUILDERS © 2015 by Johnna Adams. Reprinted by permission of Alexis Williams, Bret Adams Ltd. For performance rights, contact Alexis Williams (awilliams@bretadamsltd.net)